D0283737

THE LITTLE BOOK OF
BIG IDEAS
FOR
DADS AND DAUGHTERS

JAY PAYLEITNER
FOREWORD BY RAE ANNE PAYLEITNER

HARVEST HOUSE PUBLISHERS
EUGENE, OREGON

Cover by Bryce Williamson

Cover Image © sturti / GettyImages

Published in association with the Steve Laube Agency, LLC, 5025 N. Central Ave., #635, Phoenix, Arizona 85012.

THE LITTLE BOOK OF BIG IDEAS FOR DADS AND DAUGHTERS

Copyright © 2017 Jay Payleitner
Published by Harvest House Publishers
Eugene, Oregon 97402
www.harvesthousepublishers.com

Library of Congress Cataloging-in-Publication Data
Names: Payleitner, Jay K., author. | Payleitner, Rae Anne, author.
Title: The little book of big ideas for dads and daughters / Jay Payleitner
   and Rae Anne Payleitner.
Description: Eugene, Oregon : Harvest House Publishers, [2017]
Identifiers: LCCN 2016051409 (print) | LCCN 2017007834 (ebook) | ISBN
   9780736961981 (pbk.) | ISBN 9780736961998 (ebook)
Subjects: LCSH: Fathers and daughters—Religious aspects—Christianity. |
   Fathers and daughters.
Classification: LCC BV4529.17 .P43 2017 (print) | LCC BV4529.17 (ebook) | DDC
   248.8/421—dc23
LC record available at https://lccn.loc.gov/2016051409

Printed in the United States of America

17 18 19 20 21 22 23 24 25 / VP-JC / 10 9 8 7 6 5 4 3 2 1

WHAT ARE LITTLE GIRLS MADE OF?

*An adaption of the nineteenth-century
poem for today's young women*

Jay Payleitner

What are little girls made of?

Sugar and spice and all things nice.
Iron and lace, enchantment and grace.

Algebra rules and carpentry tools.
Beauty and brains, and horses' manes.

Freckles and braids and wild escapades.
Castles and dreams, whispers and schemes.

Wise intuition. Endless ambition.
Sweet reminisces and butterfly kisses.

That's what little girls are made of.

CONTENTS

Little Book of Big Ideas. I don't mean to contradict my father from the very first page, but a lot of these ideas aren't all that big. They are actually rather small ideas and take very little effort or time. Which conveniently matches the concise and fun-to-read nature of the book.

Some of the Big Ideas presented here may require a bit more commitment than others, but for the most part, these are not groundbreaking, wallet-busting, revolutionary strategies for being the greatest father ever. These are small, simple ideas for your everyday life. And that is where you—as a dad—can make all the difference. In the small things.

I guarantee that making a little bit of effort a hundred times is far more valuable than making a grandiose effort only a few times. I love my dad, and I trust him and value him. That's not because of big expensive vacations or mountaintop moments. And it's not because of a handful of empowering speeches mimicking something you might hear in a football locker room at halftime, or at the end of an Al Pacino movie. It's because he was there. It's because every day he would ask how my day was. He would break down my softball games with me after a tough loss. He would proofread my English papers. He would defeat me in every game of Ping-Pong, so that when I finally bested him, I knew it was well earned.

These things don't take a lot of time or brain power or money. When a dad takes a few moments every day to invest in his daughter, they add up. All those small things, all those little moments, will eventually be a big deal.

Even if you don't have all the answers, be there to listen. Even if you mess up, be there to apologize. Even if you can't stop the world from hurting your daughter, be there to hold her hand through any crisis, large or small. This is what makes for a great father. You don't have to be perfect; you just have to try. Your daughter will slowly collect and treasure your small acts of love, snippets of wisdom, bits of effort, and hints gained from experience. That is what she will take with her into the world, and that is who you will be to her.

You have the beautiful opportunity to be a lot of things to your daughter—her hero, friend, coach, confidant, and inspiration. But all of that begins quite simply with showing up and investing in the small things.

So on behalf of your daughter, I hope you find a few ideas between the covers of this book to help start you on your journey.

Dad, relax. I promise this book will be easy to read. Probably even fun. This book will not make you feel guilty, incompetent, or ignorant. The fundamental purpose of this book is for you to say, "Oh, I can do that!"

Let me also assure you that no matter how many books you read, you will never completely understand what it's like to be a girl. And that's okay. Being slightly confused and regularly surprised is actually part of the fun. Stay connected with your daughter, keep the lines of communication open, and give her lots of encouragement and confidence. Those surprises will keep coming for years to come.

Rita and I have five kids. The first four were boys. Alec,

Randall, Max, and Isaac each has his own unique personality and list of accomplishments. But as I watched their choices and adventures, I would almost always think, *Well, that makes sense.*

With our youngest, Rae Anne, my reaction to many of her choices has been, *Where did that come from?*

Rae Anne is audacious, except when she chooses to work quietly behind the scenes. She is fearless, except for a few of her secret phobias. She is a born leader with strong opinions but will gladly take advice from someone who has earned her respect. Rae wore a tiara to our local park district's daddy-daughter dance but never passed up a game of backyard football with her brothers. She was an all-state catcher in high school softball but also earned awards in speech and as a lawyer on the mock trial team. She totally surprised both Rita and me when she announced she was going to West Point. And surprised us even more when she announced she was going to law school in Dublin.

I was *not* surprised when she agreed to write the foreword for this book. She does like to share her point of view. (Thanks, Rae Anne. I love you so much.)

While Rae Anne is the inspiration for much of this book, I confess that I have been stealing ideas from other men for years when it comes to raising daughters. Hey, we dads gotta stick together. If you are inspired, challenged, or stunned by anything you read in the following pages, I'd love to hear about it. You can track me down at jaypayleitner.com.

Join the Backyard Tea Party

When you happen to look out your kitchen window and see your young daughter serving tea to a table of inanimate party guests, you already know what to do. Join the party. Even if she has not invited you, stroll out and surrender to the fantasy and frivolity. Sit crisscross applesauce on the blanket or tuck your knees up under your chin at the tiny picnic table. Chat amiably with the other guests, which may include stuffed bears and doggies, a Raggedy Ann, and an American Girl doll. Sip your "tea" daintily. Extend your pinky finger.

Little girls often create a fantasy world where all is well and only nice things happen. It's a perfectly appropriate and charming way to spend an afternoon. I believe the act of pretending is a threshold for creativity, ingenuity, resource-fulness, and even future careers and life endeavors. Hopes and dreams flourish best in a safe environment.

By the way, it may not be a tea party out the back window. If your daughter is building a Lego tower, baking mud pies, identifying cloud shapes, making up show tunes, or doing sandbox excavation with toy Caterpillar earthmoving equipment, that's all equally awesome.

"When I come home, my daughter will run to the door and give me a big hug, and everything that's happened that day just melts away."

—Hugh Jackman

BIG IDEA 2

Build a Charm Bracelet

Start this tradition on your daughter's third birthday. (Or her next one.)

Buy a sterling silver charm bracelet that's a little too big for her wrist. You can spend hundreds of dollars, but really there's no need to spend more than forty or fifty bucks. At the same time, buy four or five charms that fit her personality and yours. The first one could be a birthday cake. Another could be a heart that says something like "I love my daddy." Another could be a doggie or kitty. Buy a small silver cross for her to add to her bracelet when she turns a new corner in her Christian faith. And maybe order any other charms that demonstrate you know what's important to her or reflect interests the two of you share. Consider iconic mementos like seashells, butterflies, dinosaurs, dolphins, books, Christmas trees, the moon, flowers, footballs, angels, and so on.

The reason to get several charms right away is not to fill her bracelet all at once, but to have them ready when the time comes. Store them in a secret box in your desk, workbench, or sock drawer. It's so much easier to go to your secret stash than race to a jewelry store or remember to order a charm online.

On the other hand, when you return from a road trip, bringing home a souvenir charm proves to your daughter that you've been thinking about her. And it's one more point of connection. That tiny silver cactus, Liberty Bell, or Space Needle will initiate a conversation and maybe even a geography or history lesson inspired by your business trip to Phoenix, Philly, or Seattle. Just charming.

"I am not ashamed to say that no man I ever met was my father's equal, and I never loved any other man as much."

—Hedy Lamarr

BIG IDEA 3

Airport Skipping

You may have read the Bible verse, "Truly I tell you, unless you change and become like little children, you will never enter the kingdom of heaven" (Matthew 18:3). Preachers would suggest this instruction is telling us to be humble, trusting, free from malice, and eager to learn.

That's all true. But tapping into your inner child is also good advice for dads. A man named Patrick recalls the time he was leading his family through an airport terminal as they were moving to a different city. He held on to his six-year-old daughter's hand as they made their way to a connecting flight.

Suddenly his daughter got an excited look on her face and looked up at him. "Daddy," she said, "let's skip."

Now, you can imagine what went through his mind:

Hmmm. In dozens of flights, I've never seen a thirty-eight-year-old businessman skipping through an airport. Maybe it has happened and I just missed it, but probably not.

This was no earth-shattering moral dilemma, and yet the idea of skipping through an airport with his daughter really made him uncomfortable. Why? Are grown-ups banned from skipping? Would he see someone he knew? Would the airport etiquette police take him away on a cart with a flashing light?

But then Patrick realized maybe there was something higher at work here—higher than reputations and appearances and looking silly in public. Maybe he could pull off this one frivolous stunt, make a little girl happy, and help her forget for a few minutes that she wasn't all that excited about moving anyway.

That's what committed dads of daughters do. We put her desires above our own. Sometimes it isn't easy. We risk looking silly to put a bright spot in our daughter's day. We forego a promotion at work because it would steal too much time from our children. Maybe we put a hold on our weekend plans because little Emmie wants to go visit a space museum on a Saturday afternoon.

That isn't to say we let our children run our lives or hesitate to correct them when they need it. But maybe we should adjust our thinking so that our first thought is to give our children the desires of their hearts. I believe that's how God, our heavenly Father, responds to us.

And by the way, if you're ever walking with your young daughter through an airport terminal, feel free to be the one who initiates the skipping. It's good practice for the biblical admonition for all of us to become like a little child.[1]

Use Words

Here's an easy assignment, even for dads who are not particularly verbal.

Make frequent use of the following short phrases. Deliver them as part of your life routine. Whisper them after bedtime prayers. Text them. Say them casually to your daughter without looking up from your newspaper as she enters a room. Shout them as she heads out the door. Write them on yellow sticky notes and leave them on a book bag, purse, cereal box, bedroom door, piano, clarinet case, alarm clock, or mirror.

"There's my fabulous daughter." "Have a most excellent day!" "Nice job." "Proud of you." "That's epic!" "XXXO" "Good luck on your geography test!" "Happy half-birthday." "Good morning, beautiful!" "Study hard!" ":)" "Will you play me a song tonight?" "Looking forward to our date tonight!" "Missed you last night!" "Sorry about our argument. Love, Dad." "Thanks for being you." "I'm so glad you're my daughter." "You are a gift from God." "Love you."

Busy lives—yours and hers—can take their toll on communication. Without being intentional, you could go three or four days without any significant connection. Brief words of exhortation can bridge those gaps and might even start longer conversations. Your spoken or written encouragement will strengthen your daughter when the world tells her she doesn't matter or doesn't have what it takes.

BIG IDEA 5

Coach Her Teams

I was never a stud athlete (like you), but I have loved every moment coaching my kids in a handful of sports. Especially when they were between eight and twelve years old. At that age, you're not just playing babysitter. Most kids are coordinated enough to catch a ball and are ready for some actual instruction. Most importantly, you still know more than they do. In a few years, that might not be true.

Every year, the local youth soccer league tried to get me to coach. But I stuck to sports I knew and cared about. Wrestling, baseball, and softball.

My four years coaching young Rae Anne in softball, and later supporting her traveling softball career, may have brought us closer than anything else we experienced together.

We shared highs and lows. Victories, losses, celebrations, and frustrations. We spent lots of time in the car, dugouts, cheap restaurants, and midrange motels.

I got to see Rae at her best and at less than her best. I saw her make friends, polish skills, and develop her gifts of leadership and negotiation. She saw me laugh, teach, organize, prioritize, and get kicked out of two softball games. And she saw me apologize for my poor sportsmanship.

So if your little girl happens to join a sports team, get involved. At any level. Volunteer as a head coach, assistant, scorekeeper, equipment manager, or carpool driver. Be as close as possible for every moment of her sporting life whether that athletic career ends in early grade school or takes her into the NCAA and beyond.

Ten Differences Between Coaching Boys and Girls

1. Boys understand the pecking order. A boy sitting on the bench is more likely to accept the idea that the starters are better than him. A girl nonstarter will hold a grudge against the coach or the player who "stole" her spot, while a boy will work harder in practice to earn a starting spot.

2. Girls care about how they look in their uniform. Boys like a sharp logo and judge new uniforms by how they feel. Girls don't like pants that make their butt look big.

3. On every girls' team, at least two of the girls will hate each other. During a basketball game, one girl may literally never pass the ball to her teammate because of their animosity. Boys won't let feelings impact the game.

4. If a teammate is a jerk or loudmouth, the boys will accept him if he plays hard and makes the team better. With girls, the team chemistry would dissolve and losses would pile up.

5. Boys have pregame rituals. Girls sing in the dugout.

6. You can't schedule a girls' game or practice if there's a homecoming or prom dance that evening. With boys, it's fine.

7. A girl pitcher may cry right on the mound when she gets taken out of the game. A boy pitcher waits until he's six feet from the dugout and then chucks his glove at the watercooler.

8. When a coach directly confronts a boy about missing a pick, not tagging up on a deep fly ball, or some other neglected strategy, the boy will get mad at himself and remember the lesson. A girl thinks it's a personal attack by the coach and may miss the lesson entirely.

9. Girls often play sports for the social aspect *during* the game. Boys play sports to play sports. The social aspect for boys comes *after*—hours, days, and maybe years later.

10. Girls will efficiently shake off a tough loss and move to the next scheduled event in their busy social life. A boy will replay the turning points of the game in his head—taking much of the blame upon himself.[2]

The Difference Between Boys and Girls

There's a reason you picked up this book. You know instinctively or experientially that daughters need special attention. They're different from boys. Not better. Not worse. Just different.

Of course, all kids like ice cream and chocolate chip cookies. All kids are a little afraid of the dark, thunder, and spiders. All kids like bubbles, stuffed animals, rainbows, and piggyback rides. All kids need to learn to share, pick up their toys, and wash their hands after going potty.

But anyone who has spent significant time observing children will agree that obvious differences between boys and girls show up at a very young age. And I'm not talking about different private parts and diaper changing techniques. Or dressing them in pinks and blues.

Baby girls watch you closer. Girls talk sooner. Girls have larger vocabularies and longer attention spans. Girls use words as tools and weapons, hence the idea of "feminine wiles." Boys are more physically aggressive—more likely to grab, push, wrestle, and throw things. Girls cuddle. Boys wrestle. Girls relate. Boys explore.

Now, since every child is different, some boyish traits occasionally show up in girls. And vice versa. Some boys do talk earlier than their sisters. Some girls are natural explorers or more competitive than the boy down the street. Mass generalizations give guidance, not absolute direction.

So if you find yourself treating your daughter different than you would a son, don't assume you're being sexist or sentencing her to a second-class existence. Just the opposite! Quite often, you're discovering powerful and unique gifts and abilities that may not be found in you, her brother, the boy next door, any male classmates, or future work colleagues or dating partners.

Anytime a father intentionally engages his daughter and begins to recognize who she is and how she relates to the rest of the world, that's reason to celebrate. That little girl will grow up with an extra dose of confidence and courage. And the world needs more of that.[3]

The Magic of Stuffed Animals

Rae Anne didn't take Rags to West Point. I was kind of surprised. But then I realized she's smart enough to anticipate how much teasing (or hazing) she may have undergone if her fellow cadets found out she liked to sleep with a scraggly stuffed doggie.

Rags has been an important friend to Rae Anne for years. I know for sure she talked to Rags for a while. I'm not sure if Rags talked back, but I wouldn't be surprised at all. When Rae was maneuvering through her grade school years, the scruffy dog was never far away at bedtime. More than once, I would scoop him up and give him a voice. "Ruff, ruff, ruff. Sweet dreams, sleepyhead." I'm pretty sure my vocal interpretation did not match Rags's real voice, but Rae Anne would go along with my version. That may have laid the groundwork for future conversations when Rae Anne needed to talk to a real person with the ability to add real insight to a real problem.

When it comes to stuffed animals, I cannot imagine any father mocking or ridiculing the idea of his daughter cuddling and having pretend conversations with a fluffy toy dog, bear, penguin, giraffe, and so on. That would be a huge mistake. Even if your daughter is in high school, always respect the magic of stuffed animals. Those imaginary dialogues surely open the doors to creativity and thoughtful decision making. We adults talk to ourselves all the time. It's called thinking. Or daydreaming. Or analyzing data. It's a skill too many people don't bother to nurture.

So if you catch your daughter chatting with her polka-dot elephant, don't judge. Lean on the side of that bedroom doorway, smile warmly, and say, "What advice is old Humphrey giving you now?" That, of course, means that you have to spend enough time with your daughter to know the elephant's name.

One more thing. If you have not yet read *The Velveteen Rabbit* with your daughter, make that happen in the very near future.

Ten Awesome Names for Stuffed Animals

1. Cujo

2. Rags (as in my daughter's stuffed doggie)

3. Pillow

4. Hershey

5. Eutychus (from Acts 20:9, where a young man was so bored during one of Paul's sermons, he dozed off and fell out a third-story window)

6. (Your name), Jr.

7. Bonzo (as in the 1951 Ronald Reagan movie *Bedtime for Bonzo*)

8. Simba

9. Lunch

10. Smelly Cat

BIG IDEA 8

Totally Embarrass Her Once in a While

I happen to agree with humor columnist Dave Barry, who said, "To an adolescent, there is nothing in the world more embarrassing than a parent."

So instead of living in denial, go ahead and embrace your role as chief purveyor of awkwardness and indiscretion. Feel free to start when your daughter is in elementary school. Once a month or so, you want her to think or even say, "Dad, you're embarrassing me." That's actually a sign you're doing something right. It means you're spending some quantity time with your daughter and her friends. And it proves she cares about what you do and who you are.

Here are a few strategies that pretty much guarantee an eye roll, major blush, and pleading outburst from your school-age daughter. Lip-synching to songs playing on her iPod. Singing right along to songs playing on her iPod. Dancing of any kind. Pulling out her baby pictures. Using her secret name from when she was a toddler, like Woobie or Lolly. Wearing cargo shorts with socks that cover your calves. Kissing your wife in the kitchen. Attempting to use text lingo. Asking her girlfriends if they have boyfriends.

The lighthearted act of embarrassing your daughter turns serious as she moves through her teens, when you'll actually need to ask embarrassing questions. "Where are you going?" "What movie are you seeing?" "Who else is going?" "Can I give you twenty bucks for cab fare if you need it?" "Got your cell phone?" "You know you can call me anytime and I'll be there. For you or your friends."

My recommendation is to let these questions come out of your mouth while her friends are within earshot. As the group heads out the door or down the driveway, you actually want her to roll her eyes and say to her girlfriends, "My dad worries about me way too much." Some of the girls will say, "So does my dad." Others will stay silent, wishing their father said those things. Or maybe wishing they had a father.

Of course the goal is not really to embarrass your little girl. The goal is to stay connected to who she's becoming and what's going on in her life. By the way, embarrassing young people with your "old-fashioned" perspective is a much better choice than dressing like them, talking like them, and acting as if you're twenty years younger than you actually are. Now, that's embarrassing.[4]

Ten Awesome Stunts to Recreate with Your Daughter from When You Were a Kid

1. Run through the sprinkler. In your clothes.

2. Save a snowball in the freezer.

3. Build a fort with sofa cushions, blankets, a card table, and an upside-down laundry basket as a lookout turret.

4. Put on a puppet show with puppets... or just socks on your hands!

5. S'mores. In a campfire. Or fireplace. Or kitchen stove!

6. The classic Mentos in the Diet Coke trick.

7. Cut snowflakes from white printer paper. (Lots of folding and snipping.)

8. Build an obstacle course.

9. Hang upside down from a tree branch.

10. Pretend the floor is hot lava and jump from counters to tables to chairs.

BIG IDEA 9

Oil Her Mitt

I t's almost impossible to catch a ball with a stiff, new softball glove. Weeks before the beginning of your daughter's softball season, you'll want to invest in a reasonably priced name-brand glove—Wilson, Nokona, Miken, Mizuno—grab a bottle of leather oil, and follow the instructions.

Similarly, sharpen her skates, install a ballet bar, or erect a soccer goal in the backyard or a basketball net in the driveway. And always, always have an inflating needle handy.

One of the jobs you signed up for when you became a dad is making sure your daughter has the proper equipment, tools, and gear to help her perform at her best. You wouldn't send your son to his first baseball practice with a plastic wiffle ball bat. So please don't send your daughter to her first tennis lesson with the slightly warped wooden tennis racket you found in the attic.

While you're at it, go ahead and talk about the proper way to care for sports gear. Wiping down golf clubs. Disinfecting shin guards. Cleaning muddy cleats. Extreme heat or cold will weaken strings, leather, and plastic, so never leave gear in a car trunk for extended periods. Airing out sports gear—shoes, shin guards, helmets, batting gloves, gym bags, or anything with fabric, leather, or padding—is essential. Leaving damp gear in dark places leads to mildew, mold, and more. Drying out your equipment that's wet from rain or sweat will prevent bacteria from growing. The fact that you care enough to make sure her gear is well cared for is actually a form of encouragement to your daughter.

Finally, when your nine-year-old daughter expresses an interest in some new endeavor—sports, dance, art, fashion design, rock climbing, archery, horsemanship, filmmaking, whatever—don't spend thousands of dollars on absolute top-of-the line professional equipment. Help her get started. Cheer her progress. See if she follows through and takes care of her gear. When the time comes, you'll know whether you should invest in an $800 Dunlop Max 200g Grand Slam racket or a $12,000 Canon C300 Mark II camcorder. Until then, just remember to oil her mitt.

The next Big Idea drives home a point that may be even more important than taking care of gear. It's about taking care of each other.

"My dad drilled it in my head, you know, 'If you want it bad enough, and you're willing to make the sacrifices, you can do it. But first you have to believe in yourself.'"

—Jennie Finch,
2004 Olympic Gold Medalist, US softball

BIG IDEA 10

Have a Catch

In the movie *Field of Dreams*, Ray Kinsella (Kevin Costner) doesn't fully realize until the final scene that he had plowed under his cornfield for one reason: to play catch with his dad. You may remember the last two lines of dialogue.

"Wanna have a catch?"

"I'd like that."

Does it need to be said that girls also have a fundamental desire to have a catch with Dad? If your daughter is playing softball this summer, you have a responsibility to get her ready. If she's about nine, you even have the responsibility to teach her—if you'll excuse the expression—not to "throw like a girl."

Beyond softball, you also have the paternal privilege to help your daughter learn and master all kinds of skills. That may include making a layup and breaking ankles. A cannonball and backstroke. A bicycle kick and scoop catch. Castling and the king's gambit. Of course that means you have to actually spend time with her on a basketball court, at the pool, on a soccer field, or across a chessboard.

In many cases, you can teach her things you learned years ago. Or maybe she's involved in a sport, competition, or activity that you know nothing about. In that case, consider it an opportunity to explore, investigate, and learn together. You may be helping her find success today. Or you may be starting something the two of you can enjoy together for decades to come.

It begins when you do something as simple and rewarding as having a catch.

Go Ahead and Treat Her like a Princess

It's really okay to treat your daughter like a princess. As a matter of fact, Dad, you're the only person in the whole world who can do that. Despite what some parenting experts might say, your daughter will grow stronger and more confident every time you call her beautiful, brilliant, or "the bestest in the world." You can even call her Princess if it feels right.

She knows you're her dad. When she's little, she will love your over-the-top adulation. As she matures, she will fully comprehend that your judgment is a little biased. If you say, "You are the most beautiful girl in the world," she knows she's not. But she loves hearing that she is to you!

Just to confirm, this writer believes your daughter can

and should be a princess to you. But I also confirm, that idea won't go over so well with the rest of the world. No teacher wants to teach a princess. No boss wants to hire a princess. No knight in shining armor wants to marry a princess. A princess doesn't know how to think for herself, begin a project, finish a project, or apply for a job. She very likely can't even open a can of soup for herself. She certainly doesn't know how to fix a flat tire or tell a young squire to keep his hands to himself.

So how should you raise your princess so that she can find her place in this world? Check out the next Big Idea.

BIG IDEA 12

Raise Her as a Pioneer Woman

In her well-researched book *Strong Fathers, Strong Daughters*, Dr. Meg Meeker challenges men to raise their daughter not as a princess, but as a pioneer woman. In chapter 6, "Pragmatism and Grit," Dr. Meeker writes this:

> Princesses take. Princesses want more. Princesses demand. They expect perfection and lack pragmatism. They don't act—except to tell others what they want.
>
> But pioneer women know that life is the way it is, and they rely on themselves to move forward...
>
> Inevitably, your daughter will encounter pain. People die and loved ones get cancer. She might

not get asked to the prom. She might get pregnant at sixteen. She might develop an eating disorder. She will encounter problems, like you did. Some can be solved, some cannot. But if she is to live a substantive, healthy life, she needs to decide what to do about her problems...When princesses get bad grades, or get pregnant at sixteen, or get kicked out of school, it's always because someone else messed up; it's always someone else's fault. [5]

I stand by the previous Big Idea. Dad, you—and only you—can treat your daughter like a princess. But in relationship to every other person on the planet, raise her as a pioneer woman.

In short, that means she will grow into a woman who takes responsibility. As compared to a princess who only takes.

Your Daughter's Mom

As the father of a girl, you might think your greatest asset is your charming personality, wisdom gained through experience, hope for the future, or overflowing love. Well, you would be wrong.

All those things are quite valuable. But for most fathers, your greatest asset is the woman who gave birth to your little girl. Ideally, that's your wife, with whom you share life, love, and frequent conversations. Sometimes it doesn't work out that way. No matter what, you will increase the chances of being the dad you want to be by partnering with the woman you're thinking about right now. That's your wife, your ex-wife, your ex-girlfriend, or your daughter's mom, stepmom, favorite aunt, grandmother, and so on.

You get the point, right? You want your little girl to look up to you. But you also want her to have a woman with whom she can talk about girl stuff. Hopefully, that adult female loves your daughter nearly as much as you do. And—this may be hard—you also want someone who will hold *you* accountable when you need a gentle reminder or priority adjustment regarding your role as a dad. Wives are especially good at that if we humble ourselves and give them permission.

So no matter what, please consider your daughter's mom to be an asset, not an enemy.

"Certain is it that there is no kind of affection so purely angelic as of a father to a daughter. In love to our wives there is desire; to our sons, ambition; but to our daughters there is something which there are no words to express."

—Joseph Addison

Validate Her Heavenly Father

Y ou will never be the perfect father. You will make mistakes. But your presence is invaluable to your daughter. Just being there is more important than you may ever know. Have you heard this story?

A sweet little girl who looks a lot like your daughter is frightened by the crashes and flashes of a thunderstorm. From her bed she calls out to her daddy. He comes in with a gentle smile and sits on the edge of her bed, assuring his daughter that she need not be afraid, she is safe, and Jesus is always with her.

The little girl thinks about that idea for a moment then says, "I know that, Daddy. But right now I need someone with skin on."

You're not God. But your physical presence—your words, actions, hugs, provision, and example—is part of God's design for raising a young woman of virtue and achievement.

Years from now, you'll look back and see that even during times when you didn't know what to do or how to respond in a crisis, your presence was all that was really needed. You may have felt as if you didn't do enough. But to your daughter, you represented God with skin on.[6]

Get Her a Dog

Madison was our golden retriever. Her twelve-year life span began when Rae Anne was three, and we put that big old devoted dog to sleep when Rae was fifteen. Do you think they had a bond? Do you think Rae Anne insisted—and still does—that Madison was *her* dog? Those two had an undeniable connection.

That dog allowed my daughter to do anything. Rae Anne could watch TV using Madison as a big, furry pillow. Rae Anne would line up her stuffed dogs, expecting Madison to sit obediently, patiently, and motionless in the middle of the polyester collection. And she did.

When Rae Anne was learning to swim, Madison would race around the pool, making sure she was safe. The only time Maddie ever jumped on anyone was when they threatened Rae Anne. Sometimes Rae's brothers would pretend to attack their sister just to get the dog riled up.

Should every little girl get a dog? Probably not. But if you've got a yard and a little girl who's fascinated by dogs, I totally recommend it. Rae Anne made Madison a better dog. And Madison had a profound effect on my daughter. Love is a powerful force in any form it takes.

When it was time to put her down, I gave Rae Anne the option of waiting outside while the vet did her work. But I knew what my daughter would do. She and I sat on the floor of the vet's examining room and stroked her dog gently and thanked her for being part of our family and giving us a real-life example of unconditional love. And together Rae and I cried.

The day you bring that puppy home, take lots of photos of your new family member with your daughter. They grow so fast. The dog does too.

"No symphony orchestra ever played music like a two-year-old girl laughing with a puppy."

—Bernard Williams

The Beanbag Chat

It's a little retro, but my friend Matt suggests you get a beanbag chair and toss it into the corner of your daughter's bedroom.

She'll think it's a gift for her. But tell her it's actually your new special spot. With her permission, you might plop there once in a while—even when she's not home—to collect your thoughts, take a quick nap, or pray for her. When she is up in her room, let her know the beanbag is your special spot for sharing confidential and amiable conversations. She can invite you in. Or you should be able to knock and be welcomed in just about anytime.

If she's younger than seven, she'll love the idea. If she's ten or older, she may question your motives. At age eight and nine, who knows? Your daughter will go through stages when she is pulling you toward her one day and shutting you out the next. And that's really the point of staking some claim to a corner of her bedroom. Any chance you get to enter your daughter's world—literally—is worth the effort.

Even if you have just a few good conversations, that beanbag chair is worth the investment and risk of possible rejection. Matt told me that after one difficult conversation, during which his daughter did most of the talking, she said, "Thanks, Dad. You always make me feel better." That's a heart melter.

Last thoughts on the topic. Make sure the beanbag chair is big enough for you to crash in. And make sure it doesn't clash too much with your daughter's room decor.

Ten Things Every Girl Wants to Hear from Her Dad

1. "Thanks for the pretty drawing. Tell me about it."

2. "Let's get a puppy."

3. "Let's get a pony."

4. "You make me smile."

5. "You have so many gifts."

6. "Hey, sweetheart. Come over here and tell me about your day."

7. "I'm sorry. You were right. I was wrong. Will you forgive me?"

8. "I am so excited to see how God is going to use all your passions and talents in the next twenty years."

9. "Good night, sweet girl."

10. "I love you to the moon and back."

Crackle Her Bones

Not really. Please don't crush your daughter's skeletal system. But one dad told me he used to pick up his daughter and pretend to hug her so hard—and add crackly sound effects with his voice—that she would crumble to the floor. And they would both laugh and laugh.

I'm not sure how it started for that dad and daughter. I'm not sure how long it lasted. Maybe he'll do it with his grandkids someday. I hope so. (I've already tried it with my grandkids, and crackling their bones is quite amusing.)

BIG IDEA 18

Date Your Daughter, Part 1

Dads need to date their daughters. And daughters need to date their dads. One on one. That's the very best way to make memories and stay connected.

If most of the time you spend together is in the presence of Mom or other family members, there's a very good chance your moments of authentic connection and affection are few and far between. Mom will end up doing most of the communicating and emotional engagement. Meanwhile, Dad is doing dad stuff, which is mostly activities that do not require any relational interaction. Things like parking the car, mowing the grass, buying tickets, carrying the picnic basket, refereeing siblings, unfolding lawn chairs, yelling at umpires, assembling IKEA furniture, flipping burgers, and setting up card tables, canopies, and orange cones.

But a date is just you and her. With no distractions. And no excuses.

Now, please don't make this a burdensome problem to be solved. It's really not difficult. If she's a baby, take two minutes to nibble her toes and burble her tummy. If she's a toddler, spend ten minutes rolling in the grass, rustling in the leaves, or making snow angels. If she's five, invest a half hour. Go for ice cream. McDonald's. Find a favorite park. Take a bike ride or walk around the block. Again, it's just you and her.

Then about third grade or so, start thinking about real dates. With a plan, a time, and a destination. A movie date, lunch date, or library date. Take a class together. Coach her sports team. Or sit in the bleachers during her practices and take her out for a Slurpee after. Go window shopping. Mini golf. Disc golf. Visit a museum. Go ice skating. Visit an apple orchard. Make a pie. Go horseback riding. Go on a double date with your daughter's best friend and her dad. Go to the bank and start a savings account. Wash Mom's car. Go bowling or birdwatching. Browse a bookstore. Or just take a

Sunday drive. (Starting on page 203, you'll find a convenient checklist and just enough space to record a memory or two.)

The first reason to date your daughter is to make her feel important. She is, of course. She is just about the most important thing in your life. Your investment of just a little time and planning will confirm that fact.

Movies About Fathers and Daughters

Hollywood gets the importance of the father-daughter relationship. Some of these movies are great for watching with your daughter just for fun or to start important conversations. Others, not so much...so check the ratings and themes before popping in a DVD, downloading a movie, or strolling into a theater with your daughter.

1. *The Little Mermaid*
2. *The Descendants*
3. *Paper Moon*
4. *Fly Away Home*
5. *Armageddon*
6. *Footloose*
7. *The Princess Diaries*
8. *Beauty and the Beast*
9. *Father of the Bride*
10. *Because of Winn-Dixie*
11. *A Little Princess*
12. *Meet the Parents*
13. *Pretty in Pink*
14. *Despicable Me*
15. *Noah*
16. *We Bought a Zoo*
17. *Enchanted*
18. *Remember the Titans*
19. *The Lovely Bones*
20. *Taken*
21. *What a Girl Wants*
22. *Paul Blart: Mall Cop*

23. *I Am Sam*
24. *3 Days to Kill*
25. *Pride and Prejudice*
26. *The Vow*
27. *Dan in Real Life*
28. *Mulan*
29. *Soul Surfer*
30. *Trouble with the Curve*
31. *Crazy, Stupid, Love*
32. *Fiddler on the Roof*
33. *Dirty Dancing*
34. *On Golden Pond*
35. *To Kill a Mockingbird*
36. *Rogue One*
37. *Interstellar*
38. *The Game Plan*
39. *Three Men and a Baby*
40. *Brave*

Date Your Daughter, Part 2

Have you ever lost an entire summer? On Memorial Day you envisioned the entire months of June, July, and August stretched out before you and imagined endless adventures and jollifications. Then Labor Day came, and you realized you really hadn't gone anywhere, built anything, made any new friends, or created a single worthwhile memory. Your endless summer ended. And you had nothing to show for it.

Don't let that happen with the limited time you have with your daughter. Losing a summer is a shame. Losing those eighteen years is a tragedy of epic proportions. That's why you need to be intentional about dating your daughter. Go ahead and call them dates. Put them on your calendar. Don't let a month go by without at least one outing—usually away from home—during which you spend one-on-one time with each of your kids. But especially your daughter(s). It's a cliché, but it cannot be emphasized enough: When the house is empty, you won't believe the blur of how fast the time went.

So the second reason to date your daughter is this: Intentionally putting regular dates on your calendar guarantees you won't miss any of her amazing, ever-changing seasons of life.

"A girl's first true love is her father."

—Marisol Santiago

Date Your Daughter, Part 3

After reading the previous two Big Ideas, you might think the primary purpose of dating your daughter is to carve out some quality time for the two of you to make memories. Nope, sorry. When you take her out, the real reason you need to show up on time, open her car door, treat her with respect, and get her home on time is that you are modeling for your daughter the way any boy should act when she goes on any date at any time.

There are all kinds of jokes and stories about "rules for dating my daughter" or fathers waiting on porches with shotguns. But the truth is, you're not the gatekeeper. She is. You should expect and insist that you shake hands with any of the young suitors who might want to spend time with her.

But that's not always possible, and it's not foolproof. The best move is to help your daughter establish her own standards. And set them high.

When you're conveying to your daughter what character traits to look for in a man, feel free to use words, but your modeling will have a greater impact. For better or worse, girls tend to date and marry men *like their fathers*. Be the kind of guy you want your daughter to end up with.

Finally, when your daughter does start dating boys her own age, that doesn't mean your dates with her should stop. Actually, that's the season in life when you want to spend more time with her, not less. You may have to work a little harder to get on her busy social calendar. But if you ask nicely, she just might fit you in.

Oh, yeah...don't forget to date your wife too. That also has a positive impact on your daughter.

"Watching your daughter being collected by her date feels like handing over a million-dollar Stradivarius to a gorilla."

—Jim Bishop

Y ou may not have a driveway. Still, don't skip this Big
Idea.

You don't have to spend hours of planning and buy
tankfuls of gas to spend time with your daughter. There's a
patch of concrete or blacktop right outside your front door
(or in a nearby courtyard) that can inspire fifteen minutes or
several hours of frolicking and togetherness.

So grab a hula hoop or two. Create a sidewalk chalk art
gallery. Play jacks. Play hopscotch. Play corners or four-
square. Stickball. Practice dribbling, layups, and free throws.
Play H-O-R-S-E. Ride a unicycle. Jump rope. Skip a Fris-
bee. Brew sun tea. Blow bubbles. Play kick the can, Mother
may I?, spud, or red light, green light. Wash her bike. Wash

your car. Maybe help her set up a lemonade stand or just sit in lawn chairs and watch the cars go by.

Beyond these activities, go online for additional inspiration or see if you can recreate memories from your own youth. Driveway dates may be for just the two of you. Or you may want to rally some siblings or neighborhood kids. The grownups next door will peek out their windows and wander over, amazed that kids can still be inspired to put down their screens and play outside.

Be Wrapped Around Her Little Finger

You've probably had a friend say something like, "I'll bet your daughter has you wrapped around her little finger."

And you probably replied, "Yeah, well...maybe a little."

Despite what all the other daddy-daughter books might say, I recommend you let that happen. When she tilts her head, smiles that smile, and asks real nice, go ahead and give her just about anything she wants. You, Dad, are the only person in the world who can do that.

You might be thinking, *Jay, you're out of your mind. That's just spoiling her.* To that I respond, no, I am simply reaffirming that a relationship between a father and daughter is like no other. You would do anything for her. You know it. She knows it. Actually, she's counting on it.

Let me take that idea a step further—adding examples. You are totally committed to your daughter. You would do everything possible to protect her from harm. When she reaches her teenage years, you would chase away any boyfriends who might hurt her. Maybe even threatening them with criminal intent. If you thought she was falling way short of her abilities, you would have a serious sit-down and talk about priorities, values, and expectations. You would show up at a party where booze and drugs were flowing freely and rescue her even if it meant she might not speak to you for an entire year.

Do you see where this is going? And how it started? It's all about meeting her needs. When your little girl is little, you want her to come to you with all her requests. You'll wisely sort them out and guide her in those innocent choices. All the while, you're practicing communication and building trust. Don't worry about spoiling her. You won't. Even if she makes a few outlandish requests, you'll respond in a way that has her best interest in mind.

Think of it like this: Another way to say "She has me wrapped around her little finger" is "We're holding hands."

"Every great dream begins with a dreamer. Always remember, you have within you the strength, the patience, and the passion to reach for the stars to change the world."

—Harriet Tubman

Engage the Fads and Phases

Your daughter may lock on to a single favorite hobby or passion for her entire youth and into her adult life. Or she may go through fads and phases like wildfire.

Dolls. Barbie dolls. American Girl dolls. Raggedy Ann dolls. Legos. Superheroes. Boots. Gymnastics. Soccer. Poetry. Pez dispensers. Dogs. Cats. Ponies. Penguins. Pokemon. Purses. Vampires. Boy bands. Fad diets. Sunglasses. Choker necklaces. Toe rings. Sock monkeys. Scarves. Berets. Multiple showers per day. Hacky Sacks. Skateboards. Tattoos. Earbuds. ZhuZhu Pets.

As frightening as that sounds, you'll want to be *aware* of every phase and season. The goal is identify these trends in their earliest stages. Give it your blessing. Or help bring it to a reasonable conclusion. Or help your daughter steer around it without too much collateral damage.

Top 15 Bestselling Toys in History

1. Barbie
2. yo-yo
3. Easy-Bake Oven
4. Radio Flyer wagon
5. Silly Putty
6. Transformers
7. G.I. Joe
8. Hot Wheels
9. Etch A Sketch
10. LEGO
11. Mr. Potato Head
12. Hula Hoop
13. Star Wars action figures
14. Rubik's Cube
15. Super Soaker[7]

Two of Anything Makes a Collection

A female friend from college had a hippopotamus collection. She didn't want to have one. But when she was young, someone gave her a stuffed hippo, which she placed on a shelf next to another stuffed hippo. The collection officially began when someone noticed those two stuffed hippos and gave her a third. After a few more birthdays and souvenir-giving opportunities, well-meaning friends and relatives had delivered way too many statuettes, birthday cards, hair ribbons, pins, T-shirts, earrings, and other trinkets with a variety of hippos in a variety of poses. My gracious friend was nice about it. But I'm pretty sure she began to hate hippopotami.

The lesson for you, Dad? You may not know your daughter

as well as you think you do. She will probably not announce when she tires of her stuffed giraffe collection. You may mistakenly think her BFF is still Annie from across the street. She may no longer want to be a firefighter, ballerina, or architect. That nickname you gave her when she was four? You may need to stop calling her that. Even though you just spent $1200 on a new one, she now hates the cello. And she's decided to be a vegan.

If these attitude changes take you by surprise, you can certainly say, "When did that happen?" But please don't judge too harshly. Also, don't feel guilty for not knowing. It's a woman's prerogative to change her mind. When your daughter's mom says, "Oh, yeah. She grew out of that months ago," you can be a little perturbed. Mothers and fathers need to share information about what's going on in their daughter's life.

In any case, don't be crushed when you come back from a vacation or business trip and present your daughter with a Pez dispenser you're sure will delight her and she says, "Oh. Thanks, Dad. But I don't collect those anymore."

Your job then is to figure out what her next collection might be. Hopefully it's not boyfriends.

Two of Anything Makes a Tradition

Local park districts along the Fox River here in the Chicago suburbs have done a wonderful job connecting the towns with paved bike paths. Several years ago on a family bike riding excursion, we were about to pass an ice cream shop when my young daughter asserted, "We have to stop. It's a tradition."

Well, like any good dad, my ears are tuned to the word "tradition," so we obeyed Rae Anne's command. Even though I was pretty sure we had stopped at this particular ice cream store only a couple times before. That's when it occurred to me that a little girl's idea of tradition may be different from her father's. You and I may think that traditions go back a generation or more and are usually classic rituals and birthrights, such as carving turkeys, taking hunting trips, going to the same annual vacation spot, maintaining team allegiances, and leaving flowers on cemetery plots. But your little girl may very well place higher value on more recent memories—events and scenarios from her own short life span.

Dad, you'll want to honor that perspective. Traditions from her youth will keep your daughter connected to you through her teen years and beyond. As a matter of fact, if you want to snag the attention of your teenager, go ahead and dare to make some minor changes in a family tradition. On Independence Day, go a to different spot to watch fireworks. On Thanksgiving, try a new cranberry recipe. Put a different star on top of your Christmas tree. Your family has your own customs, and your daughter knows all of them. She may not admit it, but there's something reassuring about doing things the same way year after year. Mess with one of those protocols, and you may end up getting a stern lecture from a fifteen-year-old girl about the importance of family traditions. Take her seriously. But enjoy every word.

"To a father growing old, nothing is dearer than a daughter."

—Euripides

Ten Selfies to Take with Your Daughter

1. Sharing a banana split.

2. In the stands at an
NBA, NHL, MLB, or NFL game.

3. On a merry-go-round or roller coaster.

4. Marking a milestone. (First day of school,
new driver's license, braces off...)

5. Vacation pose. (In front of a national monument,
waterfall, canyon, or skyscraper.)

6. Pranking her sleeping brother
(or an unsuspecting houseguest).

7. In a tree.

8. Underwater.

9. Cooking breakfast in bed for Mom.

10. Puppy shopping. (Puppy purchase optional.)

Volunteer at an Animal Shelter

Without any research, I am certain that 93 percent of all middle school girls decide at one time or another to become a veterinarian. They love kitties or doggies. Even if they have never ridden a horse, they love horses and all farm animals. They may hate biology and the sight of blood. They may have no idea what vets do all day, but that's their dream job. For now.

As with all their ambitions and fantasies, your primary responsibility is to not crush their dreams. It's not helpful to say things like, "You know that takes eight years of college." "You understand that's mostly dealing with sick animals. And sometimes they die." Instead, say things that keep the door open and let her know you're on her side. "Absolutely. I could see you doing that." If the aspirations continue as they enter high school, you may want add some guidance. "Taking honors biology would be a good start."

You can actually help them move that dream toward reality or move on to the next dream by spending a Saturday at an animal shelter. There's almost certainly an establishment in your area that cares for stray and unwanted animals, and many of them are eager for volunteers. A day of cleaning out cages and listening to yips, growls, and caterwauling will be educational and eye-opening.

If you do take a shift at a local animal shelter or pound, make sure your daughter understands *ahead of time* that you will not be taking home a creature to call your own that day. That is not a decision to make on the spur of the moment. If you want to identify a potential adoptee and place a hold on the little varmint, that's fine. Give yourself at least twenty-four hours to make a reasoned decision.

Dedicate Something to Her

There are all kinds of ways to memorialize your devotion for your daughter. If possible, I recommend you dedicate something to her that has artistic, architectural, educational, poetic, or literary value. Be creative. More than one housing developer has snuck a Rachel Avenue or Megan Boulevard into a new neighborhood. *Lindsay* or *Kaitlin* is certainly a better name for your yacht than *Seas the Day* or *Breakin' Wind*.

Dave Thomas named his fast-food restaurant chain after his daughter Wendy. In 1949, bakery entrepreneur Charlie Lubin named his cheesecake after his eight-year-old daughter, Sara Lee. An Austrian businessman, one of the first customers of automotive pioneers Gottlieb Daimler and Karl Benz, placed an order for thirty-six custom-designed cars, insisting they be named for his daughter Mercedes.

Billy Joel wrote "Lullabye (Goodnight My Angel)" for his daughter Alexa Ray. Stevie Wonder composed "Isn't She Lovely?" for his daughter Aisha.

P.G. Wodehouse wrote a collection of short stories titled *The Heart of a Goof* and whimsically dedicated it, "To my daughter Leonora without whose never-failing sympathy and encouragement this book would have been finished in half the time." Talk show host Jimmy Fallon wrote a children's book titled *Your Baby's First Word Will Be Dada*, and of course, he dedicated it, "For Winnie, who made me a Dada." Roald Dahl's 1982 children's classic *The BFG* begins with a heartbreaking dedication to his daughter:

For Olivia
20 April 1955—17 November 1962

Without comparing myself to any of these authors, allow me to confirm that my book *52 Things Daughters Need from Their Dads* was dedicated, "To Rae Anne. You brighten each day." She knows what that means.

In the course of your vocation or avocation, is there a place where you can honor your daughter? Maybe it's not for the world to see, but simply a meaningful image or icon, or her initials situated in just the right place. For example, a smiling photo tucked up in a trucker's visor or as a screensaver on your laptop. You could have her initials inscribed on a coin or key chain you carry in your pocket. It's not my style, but you may consider sitting for a tattoo of your daughter's name or initials. Or maybe, like astronaut Gene Cernan, you could etch your daughter's initials in lunar dust if you ever travel to the moon.

Dad, I know you think of your daughter often. Hundreds of times per day. You pause, picture her beautiful face, and pray for her well-being. But she doesn't know that. The real reason to make an obvious and clear statement that she means the sun, moon, and stars to you is not to remind you. It's to remind her.[8]

Ten Memorable Fathers and Daughters in Literature

1. Lizzy Bennett and Mr. Bennett
Pride and Prejudice, Jane Austen, 1813

2. Anne Frank and Otto Frank
The Diary of Anne Frank, Anne Frank, 1947

3. Cosette and her adopted father, Jean Val Jean
Les Miserables, Victor Hugo, 1862

4. Scarlett O'Hara and Gerald O'Hara
Gone with the Wind, Margaret Mitchell, 1936

5. Scout Finch and Atticus Finch
To Kill a Mockingbird, Harper Lee, 1960

6. Liesel Meminger and her adopted father, Hans Hubermann
The Book Thief, Markus Zusak, 2006

7. Cordelia and King Lear
King Lear, William Shakespeare, 1606

8. Matilda Wormwood and Mr. Wormwood
Matilda, Roald Dahl, 1988

9. Eliza Doolittle and Alfred P. Doolittle
Pygmalion, George Bernard Shaw, 1912

10. Nancy Drew and District Attorney Carson Drew
The Nancy Drew Mystery Stories, Carolyn Keene.
The first volume, *The Secret of the Old Clock*,
was published in 1930.

Dating Warning

There's a story about a man who had three lovely daughters. As they began dating, this father was delighted that every boy who came to their door was pleasant and well mannered. One day he casually mentioned to his oldest daughter that he truly liked all the young men she and her sisters brought home.

With a hint of an impish smile, the young lady replied, "You know, Daddy, we don't show you everybody."

It's a cute story. But it contains a warning dads need to heed. Your lovely daughter may never lie to you. But there's a 100 percent chance she's not going to tell you everything that's going on in her life. Which is probably a good thing. You don't *want* to know everything. But you do need to know enough to be able to protect her from things that can harm her physically and emotionally. Especially any altercations and tragic decisions that leave lasting scars.

Be aware of any time she might be heading toward a dangerous precipice. Whenever possible, rescue your daughter at the top of that cliff or slippery slope. Grab her. Hug her tight. Before she goes over the edge.

BIG IDEA 29

Surrender to the American Girl Phenomenon

I'm not shilling for American Girl. They're doing pretty well without my help. I'm just saying that dolls and dads *can* mix. And the backstories on almost all American Girl dolls can lead to valuable history lessons. Felicity grew up during the American Revolution. Addy is a fugitive slave during the Civil War. Kit lived through the Great Depression. Molly's life reflects the patriotism of the World War II era. And in many cases, the fathers of these fictional girls are also pretty good role models for dads.

The top-ten most popular American Girl dolls are...

1. Samantha Parkington

2. Molly McIntire

3. Kirsten Larson

4. Felicity Merriman

5. Kit Kittredge

6. Elizabeth Cole

7. Emily Bennett

8. Ivy Ling

9. Rebecca Rubin

10. Julie Albright

If you and your daughter dive into this world, here's some free advice. Don't go overboard. You can drop big bucks in a hurry on all kinds of outfits and accessories. So if you and your daughter are browsing their catalogs or website, or if you've trekked to one of their stores, you'll want to treat each purchase as a teachable moment.

Think of it as setting some ground rules for the next decade. If she really wants the gingham jumper and the plaid sweater vest with matching skirt for Molly, respectfully suggest she choose one outfit or the other. If she simply must have the accessory pack, three adventure books, and the DVD, say

"No, I don't think so" and then secretly order those items and tuck them away for Christmas or her next birthday. If she throws herself on the floor of the store screaming that she can't live without the entire wardrobe and absolutely every Molly accessory, leave immediately and without apology.

Worth mentioning. American Girl corporate decisions have sparked controversies over the years, and some even led to boycotts. As a dad, you'll have to decide whether you want to contribute to the profits of a company that may not fully share your values. That's also a conversation to have with your daughter. It's good practice, Dad. Until the Lord returns, the world in which your daughter is growing up is only going to get more and more complicated.

"Little girls love dolls. They just don't love doll clothes. We've got four thousand dolls, and ain't one of them got a stitch of clothes on."

—Jeff Foxworthy

My Little Pony, Build-A-Bear, Webkinz, Barbie, the Powerpuff Girls, and So On

Along with American Girl paraphernalia, dads should expect to see a constant stream of dolls, toys, and stuffed animals targeted at that little female consumer you are raising. Most of these playthings are harmless except for their ability to instigate young girls to beg their parents to spend lots of money. This Big Idea will include no judgment or reviews about any specific products. Only recommendations and warnings for dads.

I recommend you allow *some* of this stuff into your house. Yes, you're opening the door to a corporate marketing machine beginning to mold your unsuspecting daughter into a longtime customer. Their well-researched game plan is to convince her that if she doesn't have the latest version with all the accessories, then she's not part of the "in crowd." And make no mistake, even young girls want to be part of the "in crowd." That's why an involved dad needs to be vigilant. You are the best person to help her learn that often, less really is more.

Follow your daughter's lead, observing her interests and curiosities. If she expresses a desire to own some of the current favorites, don't tell her she's been duped by the corporate industrial complex and that she's a fool for being influenced by such nonsense. Hey, she's a little girl and wants to play make-believe with her friends. Instead, begin training her to manage her desires and practice sound judgment. Those skills will come in handy throughout her life.

So—on a special occasion or "just because"—go ahead and splurge on one of the characters, dolls, or stuffed animals she has been hinting or asking about. Not ten items. Not an entire roomful of outfits, accessories, and matching BFF dolls and animals. But just enough for her to appreciate, take care of, and not take for granted.

With one doll and one (or maybe two) outfits, she'll think, *This is awesome!*

With the next purchase, she'll think, *This is nice.*

And the enthusiasm diminishes from there.

Put another way: Making a few modest purchases makes you a hero, which is always a good thing. Dropping a few hundred bucks for a spoiled child makes you a chump, which is *not* such a good thing.

By submitting to the marketing pressure and investing in one or two of these popular toys for girls, you are also securing another chance to gain and build your daughter's trust. Here's what I mean. One of your biggest fathering roles is protector. When you first held that new baby girl, you made a promise to protect her from obvious things like starvation, sunburn, boys, and monsters under the bed. But worse than all of those threats is the humiliation of being rejected or judged harshly by her peers.

I heard the story a father who tried to protect his daughter from the dangers of consumerism by buying her a knock-off doll from a discount store. The girl hid her disappointment and politely accepted the gift. But then came an invitation to a party where she knew every other third-grade girl would bring the more expensive name-brand doll. Suddenly this girl didn't want to go to the party. The mom and dad forced her to go, saying, "It'll be fine. No one will notice." But it wasn't fine. The other girls—mean ones—did notice. And the trauma was more than any third-grade girl should have to handle.

You can say it was a good lesson and those other girls weren't worthy of being her friends anyway. But this little girl was not prepared to fight that battle. That day her desperate need to always possess the latest consumer fad *increased* dramatically. Which was the exact opposite of her father's goal.

All that to say, Dad, fight the battles that really matter. And make sure you do everything possible so that your daughter knows you are on her side.

Ten Most Popular Names for Baby Girls in 1920

1. Mary
2. Dorothy
3. Helen
4. Margaret
5. Ruth
6. Mildred
7. Virginia
8. Elizabeth
9. Frances
10. Anna

BIG IDEA 31

Those Not-So-Nice Toys

Video games are getting darker and creepier. While they seem to be marketed more heavily toward boys and young adult males, don't assume your daughter is immune. Consider yourself warned.

Beyond electronic games, every year the market also welcomes a questionable array of dolls, games, and other toys that are inappropriate for all kinds of reasons. They encourage violence, blasphemy, profanity, cult activity, promiscuity, and so on.

In 2016, Mattel made history by introducing two new variations of the classic Barbie figure—curvy Barbie and petite Barbie. Still, fashion dolls give girls an impossible role model of the female figure, leading to all kinds of self-image challenges.

Without giving examples, let's also admit that quite a few books, music, movies, television, and other media give nightmares to caring dads everywhere. What's a dad to do?

As we mentioned in Big Idea 30, items that are morally neutral can be enjoyed in moderation. But we do need to protect our young daughters from dangerous or evil influences. Then, as they get older, we equip them to make responsible decisions on their own. We demonstrate the value of seeking a higher moral ground. We encourage our girls to follow the biblical admonition, "Whatever is true, whatever is noble, whatever is right, whatever is pure, whatever is lovely, whatever is admirable—if anything is excellent or praiseworthy—think about such things" (Philippians 4:8).

That sounds pretty straightforward, doesn't it? Let's help our daughters fill their minds with only good stuff. But we can't stop there. Allow me to share two other verses that will help clarify our task and remind us of our responsibility.

At the Last Supper, Jesus offers a prayer for his disciples, asking his Father in heaven to allow them to live safely even though there is evil in the world. "My prayer is not that you take them out of the world but that you protect them from the evil one. They are not of the world, even as I am not of it" (John 17:15-16).

That passage suggests that while our family is here on earth, we can't hide from Satan. But with Jesus' help, we can stand up to him.

Jesus also delivered a warning that seems especially valid for fathers who need a clear reminder to safeguard their daughter from Satan's tempting. He said, "It would be better for them to be thrown into the sea with a millstone tied around their neck than to cause one of these little ones to stumble" (Luke 17:2). Men, let's all pledge to do our best to keep our little ones from stumbling.

If it feels as if you're doing battle with the world when it comes to protecting your daughter, you're exactly right. But the Bible has good news for those who know Christ. He has promised to be an invincible partner in the battle. "In this world you will have trouble. But take heart! I have overcome the world" (John 16:33).

BIG IDEA 32

The Boy Band Conundrum

In my mind, they all blend together: Backstreet Boys, NSync, New Kids on the Block, Jonas Brothers, and so on. Are they evil forces that drag young girls into the dark recesses of hell? Probably not. Are they brilliant creative geniuses worthy of worship? Definitely not.

Every generation of teenyboppers welcomes its own version of the boy band. Typically a corporate music producer assembles a few good-looking boys who can carry a tune and follows the prearranged blueprint to make them pop stars. The costumes, promotional tours, formulaic songs, singable harmonies, and mild scandals all lead to non-acoustical stadiums filled with screaming preteen girls.

Sometimes those girls are accompanied by their perceptive and prudent dads. And that's the point.

When your daughter becomes starry eyed and starts putting up posters of the next boy band, don't freak out. Yes, some of their bouncy or soulful songs will hint at sexual encounters. On the posters, one or all of the young men will have their airbrushed six-pack abs exposed. One of the band members will be labeled a "renegade bad boy" and may be linked in the tabloids with a young starlet who also happens to be looking for publicity. The talent agents, music promoters, and public relations experts have worked it all out. Your daughter will read about it on various social media sites and be devastated that her heartthrob crush is dating such a tramp.

Dad, I think you know what you have to do. When the tour comes through your area, buy two tickets and take your little girl. Maybe buy three or four tickets and have your daughter invite her closest friends. You'll be a hero. You'll make sure she gets home safe. And you'll have earned the right to talk with her in the future about music, lyrics, boys, love, friends, and entertainment choices.

Escorting your young daughter to a pop music concert or

any creative venue that may deliver less than savory content is a wise move for any dad. You'll want to do a bit of research. If the creative content turns really creepy, then model the act of leaving the premises. But it will probably all turn out fine as long as you're there to help sort out the fun stuff from the stuff that's a little naughty and then help her put it all in perspective. Years from now, your daughter will be confronted with much worse, and she'll be more likely to make good decisions because you had the courage and foresight to help shape her values and worldview when she was just a kid.

"I want the men everywhere to pray, lifting up holy hands without anger or disputing. I also want the women to dress modestly, with decency and propriety."

—1 Timothy 2:8-9

Ten Things Daughters Will Never Hear from Their Dad

1. "Take my card. The bank just raised my credit limit."

2. "Curfew, schmurfew!"

3. "We've only set aside $40,000 for your wedding."

4. "Love all your new piercings."

5. "Can't decide? Buy all three pair."

6. "I signed up to coach your ballet team."

7. "I gave your cell phone number to that guy on the Harley with the bandana, earrings, and face tattoo."

8. "Oh look, a GAP! I can wait if you want to go try on a few things."

9. "Daytona Beach for spring break? Sounds like fun! Go for it."

10. "Happy sixteenth birthday. Your new Jaguar is in the driveway."

BIG IDEA 33

Do What Moms Do

You're a man's man. No doubt about it. You kill spiders. You read the sports page. Because you're secure in your manliness, you're not even afraid to hold your wife's purse when she's in the department-store dressing room.

Take that testosterone and virility and set it aside long enough to do some girl stuff. If you're looking for something out of the ordinary to do on your next date with your daughter, try taking a class or attending an event that would typically include almost exclusively women.

Examples? Ceramics. Pottery painting. Jewelry making. Calligraphy. Stained glass. Bonsai gardening. Poetry writing. Poetry reading. Linoleum block printmaking. Basketry. Pastry creations. Cake decorating. Watercolor painting. Metal crafting. Woodcarving. Papermaking. Weaving. Storytelling.

You get the idea. Go online and see what classes your local park district or craft store has to offer. Check the weekend guides in your local newspaper. When you show up with your daughter, you should expect a little pushback as well as a bit of appreciation from other attendees. Some may think you're crashing a girls-only event. Others will be delighted that a man is investing in his daughter. One option would be to sign up as a foursome with your daughter's best friend and her father.

Before committing to a class that goes eight weeks or more, you may want to try a single-event workshop. But no matter what, go ahead and totally surrender to the idea. Be the best darn pastry chef you can be. Cut that stained glass with precision. Weave a potholder to be proud of. If your clay pot explodes in the kiln or your watercolor drips, really, it's okay. The memories you're making will be even sweeter.

Finally, if you're in a calligraphy, printmaking, or paper-making class, bring home something macho and inspirational to hang on your wall. May I suggest...

Iron sharpens iron.

Proverbs 27:17

Every man dies. Not every man lives.

William Wallace

If you're going through hell, keep going.

Winston Churchill

"Think what cowards men would be if they had to bear children. Women are an altogether superior species."

—George Bernard Shaw

BIG IDEA 34

Treat Her like a Son

I don't know how many kids you have. (I assume you have at least one daughter because you're reading this book.) But there's a good chance, if you have a son, there are occasions when you naturally welcome him into some aspect of your life simply because he's a guy and you're doing guy stuff. You didn't plan it. But if you look back at the last week or last month, you might realize that you spent time with your son watching or playing sports, doing yard work or other chores, or introducing him to your own hobbies because it felt comfortable passing your interests on to another male.

Well, first of all, don't feel guilty. Father-son stuff is important. But second, slap your forehead and say right out loud, "Holy cow! Of course my daughter can do all that stuff!" She can watch football, play golf, fish, mend fences, plant sod, shoot a paintball gun, build a ship in a bottle, or find the Orion Nebula with a telescope.

There are still a few things that may be just guy stuff, but not many.

Worth noting, the younger you invite your daughter (or son) to join you in a chore or hobby, the more eager they will be. Young kids really just want to hang out with their dad. If and when their interest wanes, don't feel abandoned or disappointed. After all, you want them to follow their *own* gifts and passions. The time spent with you may open the door to some long-term interest or vocation, or it might just be time getting to know their old man. No regrets.

Do Stuff with Your Son and Daughter

I'm a huge proponent of one-on-one time with kids. Maybe because Rita and I have five kids, and any time spent with just one child was rare and precious. When it's just you and your daughter, there's finally a chance to talk about things that are really important. Big brother won't make fun of what she's trying to say. Little brother won't interrupt with some goofy outburst, looking for attention. I encourage all dads to plan and cherish one-on-one time.

But my friend Chassyn, who grew up in upstate New York, reminded me that father-son-daughter time is pretty special too. She fondly remembers sitting with her younger brother while Dad shouted at the Bills or Sabres on TV. He often took them both fishing, and all three played catch in the backyard. When their father shared wisdom, brother and sister were both right there to soak it up. They competed, trying to impress Dad by being the first to identify the make and model of vehicles on the road just by their headlights or taillights. That's a skill she learned from her dad and can't stop doing to this day.

Having welcomed another generation, the entire family is still tight, and Chassyn credits her father. What makes her story even more special is the fact that Chassyn is a stepdaughter to this man who loves her so much. A fact she didn't even know until she was almost a teenager.

So be a one-on-one dad. Be a son-plus-daughter dad. Be an all-in-this-together dad. And if the circumstance comes up, be a dad who treats your kids, stepkids, adopted kids, foster kids, and so on all the same. The more, the merrier.

"He opened the jar of pickles when no one else could. He was the only one in the house who wasn't afraid to go into the basement by himself. He cut himself shaving, but no one kissed it or got excited about it. It was understood when it rained, he got the car and brought it around to the door. When anyone was sick, he went out to get the prescription filled. He took lots of pictures...but he was never in them."

—Erma Bombeck

Ten Unexpected Places to Take Your Daughter (That Really Shouldn't Be Unexpected)

1. a hardware store
2. a local high school football game
3. car dealerships
4. historical sites
5. a planetarium or observatory
6. a driving range
7. a shooting range
8. a music store
9. camping
10. hiking, geocaching, spelunking, or mountaineering

Things Not to Talk About

Following are things that your daughter probably will not bring up with you. If she does, I would be quite surprised. Feel free to say at any time, "I think your mother may have a bit more wisdom in this area than me."

Puberty. Menstruation. Facial hair. Body hair. Acne. Body odor. Cramps. PMS. Bras. Feminine hygiene products. Gynecological exams. Her first crush. Her first kiss. Her first broken heart.

Now, it's possible some of these issues may come up. Especially with single dads. If your daughter does begin a conversation about personal hygiene or early dating relationships, I recommend you do more listening than talking. When the conversation is over, make sure she is glad she came to you for comfort and advice. In the meantime, stand ever ready to make a late-night run to Walgreens, give a male perspective when asked, or offer a shoulder to cry on when the world doesn't seem fair.

"The father of a daughter is nothing but a high-class hostage. A father turns a stony face to his sons, berates them, shakes his antlers, paws the ground, snorts, runs them off into the underbrush, but when his daughter puts her arm over his shoulder and says, 'Daddy, I need to ask you something,' he is a pat of butter in a hot frying pan."

—Garrison Keillor

Value Her Opinion

Admitting that men and women tend to have different perspectives and opinions is healthy. But an ongoing theme of this book is that every child is unique, which means it's critical we stay away from putting our daughter (or son) in a box with a label based solely on their gender. Sweeping generalizations insisting that girls do things one way and boys do things another way are not surprising. Those stereotypes are typically not helpful.

Somehow a dad needs to let his daughter know that it's okay to play with dolls, cry at movies, sing in the kitchen, like kitties, and follow her desire to nurture. But that same dad also needs to let his daughter know that it's okay for her to play with trucks, excel at sports, like action films, and be good at science and math. Your daughter needs to build her identity around her relationship with God and her own gift-edness and accomplishments.

So how do you treat her like a girl but also reaffirm that she doesn't have to be a fashion model, a boy toy, or a helpless damsel in distress? She needs to know she can have her own opinions. She can be competitive and fight for her rights. She can be a strong leader without being a radical feminist. She can be feminine without being a pushover.

Fathers may have a unique ability to help in this area. You're a boy, she's a girl. Same family, different perspectives. One strategy for fathers may be to confirm that her opinion has value. It may very well be different from yours. But that doesn't make it wrong or right.

As an aside: We're not talking about matters of integrity or character. Don't budge on the moral absolutes important to your family and faith. The Ten Commandments turn out to be a handy reference in this regard.

The secret may be—starting at an early age—to ask your daughter's opinion. That can be informative and empow-ering. Even a third grader has opinions about style, design, colors, vacation destinations, restaurant choices, television shows, video games, and favorite hockey players. Suggesting that her opinions have value and don't have to match yours can be a stunning and important revelation to your daughter. Some examples may help. Imagine asking your daughter...

- "For Christmas, should I get Mom the amethyst earrings or the opal ones?"

- "Dalmatian, golden retriever, or Weimaraner?"

- "On our last day in Orlando...Magic Kingdom or Epcot?"

- "What should we do for Grampa's birthday this year?"

- "We need some new patio chairs. What are your thoughts?"

- "I'm designing a flyer for the block party—can you take a look at this font?"

- "A guy I work with wants to recommend some summer reading for his daughter who's eight. Any ideas?"

- "iPad or Chromebook?"

In some cases, you can narrow down your choices and invite your daughter to answer a simple either/or question.

That way her answer is already welcome. In some areas, she may actually have much more insight than you. Open up a question for discussion, and she may help you come up with a decision you may have never considered.

The goal is to empower her. Asking your daughter's opinion—and sometimes even engaging her in healthy debate—confirms that she can be herself. Taking it one step further, that gives her the responsibility to think things through, do the research, develop rational opinions based on fact, and listen to both sides of an argument.

How can you fight stereotypes and sweeping generalizations about gender? On one hand, avoid putting any child in a box. On the other hand, don't deny the differences between girls and boys. Instead, help your daughter develop and celebrate her own perspective, preferences, and identity.

Listen to Yourself Speak

Guys notice pretty girls. That's how God wired us. But even if we notice, we need to be intentional about holding those thoughts in check. Maybe just as important—especially for dads driving with little girls in the backseat—we need also to hold our tongues. I know you would never say anything like, "Whoa, check out that hottie!" or "Hubba-hubba! Too bad I'm married!" But you might let thoughts slip out like, "You can tell she works out," or "How did that pretty girl end up with a geeky-looking guy like that?"

At a very young age, girls become aware of how the world values slender girls with all the right curves. If your spoken words confirm that idea, you need to take several steps back and carefully consider what you are telling your daughter.

Fathers need to realize that this self-image challenge is beyond our male experience. You and I have never been a girl sifting through the oppressive cultural forces that judge how we look. It's more devastating than most guys can ever imagine. Even some girls who might be considered perfectly proportioned and beautiful in the eyes of the world will hate what they see in the mirror.

And again, Dad, your words matter. That means you cannot say many of the things you believe are harmless or even helpful. Innocent phrases *do* harm and *don't* help. Examples: "Are you getting enough exercise?" "Why don't you eat an apple instead?" "It's funny how your sister can eat so much and doesn't put on any weight." "Did you know there are 140 calories in a can of Coke?" "My Aunt Ruth was overweight."

None of these sounds like an attack. But if any of those come out of your mouth, your lovely, sweet, and perfect little girl is going to hear this: "Daughter, you're fat." If that sounds harsh, that's because it *is* harsh. Very harsh. If you don't believe me, ask your wife.

Finally, let's take this a step further. Yes, you need to watch your words. But you might also literally have to change the way you think. Choose to see people through the eyes of God. The Bible confirms, "The LORD does not look at the things people look at. People look at the outward appearance, but the Lord looks at the heart" (1 Samuel 16:7).

When your daughter looks in the mirror, she needs to see someone cherished by God. And loved unconditionally by her earthly father too.

Ten Things your Daughter Needs to Know Before She Leaves Home

1. How to do laundry.

2. Too much fast food isn't good for your tummy, health, or wallet.

3. Pay credit cards off every month.

4. Anything posted online may be seen by future bosses or boyfriends.

5. Getting up for church on Sunday morning starts your week off right. (And reminds you to wind down your Saturday nights a bit earlier as well.)

6. Be on time. Meet deadlines. Take responsibility.

7. Read the manuals. (Including God's Word.)

8. Do what's right, not what's easy.

9. If you pose for too many pictures, the world will pass you by.

10. You can always come home. Always.

Her Number One Need

My colleagues at the National Center for Fathering are well known for their meticulous research that helps dads know how to connect with their children and be the dad God calls men to be. One of the more eye-opening insights came when they asked a significant number of girls to write an anonymous response to this statement concerning their dads: "I wish you would _____."

One theme emerged in an overwhelming number of responses—*listening*. As you read these transcribed responses, see if you can hear your daughter's voice.

> "I wish my dad would try and understand what I'm going through, and be there when I need

someone to talk to just as a friend and not as a parent."

"I need him to completely hear me out and not assume things…to listen before he speaks."

"Take time and not talk but let me tell him one secret that I have hidden for a long time."

"Try to see where I'm coming from before blowing up in my face and later wanting my forgiveness."

"Listen when I need you to. You don't have to have the right answers all the time; just be there for me."

"I wish my dad would just listen to me and not try to make everything about him."

"If my dad would listen and forgive me without always a punishment, I would open up and tell him more! I don't because I'm scared of getting grounded."

"Actually stop and listen…don't think about what you're going to say, but hear and understand what I'm saying."

"I wish he would speak calmly, not in a tone of voice that scares me."

"Listen to me [without trying] to fix the problem or discipline me for it, but just listen."

"Don't talk; don't argue; just listen."

There were many more similar responses, but you get the point. So did you hear your daughter's voice? If you didn't, then you *really do* need to work on your listening skills.[9]

"Jesus turned and saw her. 'Take heart, daughter,' he said, 'your faith has healed you.' And the woman was healed at that moment."

—Matthew 9:22

Lessons from the Animals

Just about every little girl likes animals. A wise father will take advantage of that idea to help his little girl see that God will give her sure footing even in high places, carry her close, provide her every need, equip her for hard work, prepare her for battle, and help her soar. Scripture writers often used animal references to get their point across.

- "It is God who arms me with strength and keeps my way secure. He makes my feet like the feet of a deer; he causes me to stand on the heights" (Psalm 18:32-33).

- "He tends his flock like a shepherd: He gathers the lambs in his arms and carries them close to

135

his heart; he gently leads those that have young" (Isaiah 40:11).

- "I tell you, do not worry about your life, what you will eat or drink; or about your body, what you will wear. Is not life more than food, and the body more than clothes? Look at the birds of the air; they do not sow or reap or store away in barns, and yet your heavenly Father feeds them. Are you not much more valuable than they? Can any one of you by worrying add a single hour to your life?" (Matthew 6:25-27).

- "Go to the ant, you sluggard; consider its ways and be wise!" (Proverbs 6:6).

- "The horse is made ready for the day of battle, but victory rests with the LORD" (Proverbs 21:31).

- "Those who hope in the LORD will renew their strength. They will soar on wings like eagles" (Isaiah 40:31).

Digging deeper into the Bible, you'll find stories of a talking donkey, a giant fish, a shepherd boy who slew a lion, and a lying serpent in the Garden of Eden.

At Christmastime, you may want to open to Luke, chapter 2, and give credit to the donkey Mary rode from Nazareth to Bethlehem and the animals surrounding the newborn Jesus.

> Joseph also went up from the town of Nazareth in Galilee to Judea, to Bethlehem the town of David, because he belonged to the house and line of David. He went there to register with Mary, who was pledged to be married to him and was expecting a child. While they were there, the time came for the baby to be born, and she gave birth to her firstborn, a son. She wrapped him in cloths and placed him in a manger, because there was no guest room available for them (Luke 2:4-7).

The passage never specifically mentions any animals. But Joseph wouldn't have made his pregnant wife walk those 111 kilometers. And since Jesus' first crib was a feed trough, there were certainly farm animals nearby.

Dads and daughters getting to know our heavenly Father with the help of scores of animals mentioned in the Bible...now *that's* a Big Idea.

BIG IDEA 41

Sports! Or Not

Tons of dads connect with their daughter through athletics. Cheering, coaching, watching, strategizing, and so on. But not all daughters do sports. And not all dads do sports.

Still, if at all possible, your little girl should spend at least a couple seasons on a local park district soccer team. Or maybe tumbling. Or some low-expectation physical activity that just about every kid in town experiences for a summer.

Like so many things, she needs to try sports. She needs to test her skills and abilities. She needs to test her competitive drive and killer instinct. (Of course, she may not have that particular gene, and that's okay.) Your daughter needs to have at least a couple pages in her scrapbook filled with team photos and participation ribbons to prove she once was part of a group of small children who had no clue about what it means to be a sweeper, point guard, or shortstop.

Give her a taste of ice skating, dance, gymnastics, golf, or swimming. Have her try some sports that are totally outside your area of expertise. You never know.

If she doesn't express any interest or talent, then back off, Dad. Your daughter does not have to play sports. The local traveling and varsity teams will do just fine without her. And you have the privilege of joining your daughter as she explores a gazillion other options when it comes to hobbies, artistic pursuits, and other extracurricular activities.

The truth is that by high school, the commitment to a sport may suck up twenty hours per week. Imagine what your daughter could do with that amount of time if she devoted it to songwriting, poetry, sculpting, magic, ballet, debate, theater, illustration, software programming, robotics, pastry making, oil painting, architecture, and so on.

Plus, some of those nonsport activities still present opportunities to compete, lead, travel, and experience teamwork.

Which means that many of the wonderful skills learned in athletics can be acquired in other venues.

Again, your daughter does not have to play sports. If she chooses not to, part of your job is to make sure she invests her newly reclaimed time in something other than texting, Snap-chatting, mani-pedis, and video games.

Ten Ways to Nurture
Your Daughter's Creative Gifts

1. Encourage her to try piano lessons.

2. Introduce her to the local children's theater.

3. Build or buy an art easel.

4. Keep Play-Doh handy.

5. Consider ballet, tap, or jazz lessons.

6. Take her to storytelling time at the local library.

7. Let her try out a potter's wheel.

8. Check out CAD for kids.

9. Launch a family blog.

10. Buy a few books of jokes, riddles, and trivia.

The Clothes Shopping Opportunity

Going shopping for clothes with your daughter might sound like a torturous expedition for both of you. But with a little patience and a thoughtful approach, a few hours in a mall with your favorite young lady might be a springboard for a new season of growth and communication in your relationship. Let's consider some of the practical life lessons you may be able to convey.

Give her a budget. Be generous. But set a limit. That's going to force her to make smart buying decisions. Should she get two pairs of jean shorts or a single, more expensive pair? Adults make that kind of decision all the time, and that's a skill your daughter needs to learn.

If she's adding to her summer wardrobe, then you have

the opportunity and obligation to provide input about what's appropriate for a girl to wear. Make no mistake—it's essential for us to be proactive in this area and intentional about influencing our daughters toward modesty. We all know what guys are thinking when they see young ladies in revealing outfits, and we need to talk to our daughters about that. Maybe even telling them they're sending a message they don't want to send.

Don't have the conversation in the store. But later, in the car or over ice cream, a dad should be able to talk with his daughter about what scenarios may unfold when a woman flaunts her body or doesn't respect herself. Reaffirm your family's values. Let her know that what the culture says is in style often doesn't line up with God's Word. Dad, you are the right person to address those issues with your daughter.

Finally, your shopping trip can also be a chance for you to learn a few things.

- What's in fashion and who says so? This question tells you what voices your daughter is listening to.

- What's on your daughter's social calendar in the coming weeks? This provides topics for future conversations and helps you know what's going on in her life.

- How's your daughter's self-image? When she's trying on clothes, is she overly worried about her looks or her body type?

- What items did she really want but were over her budget? You can pick them up later as birthday or Christmas presents.

- What might be a stylish gift you could pick up for your wife? Your daughter will have ideas you would never even consider.

Dad, anytime you can enter your daughter's world, do it. An afternoon of shopping has all kinds of possible benefits. Just make sure your credit card is primed and ready to go.

"It is admirable for a man to take his son fishing, but there is a special place in heaven for the father who takes his daughter shopping."

—John Sinor

"Your beauty should not come from outward adornment, such as elaborate hairstyles and the wearing of gold jewelry or fine clothes. Rather, it should be that of your inner self, the unfading beauty of a gentle and quiet spirit, which is of great worth in God's sight."

—1 Peter 3:3-4

Imagine Your Daughter's Future Husband

A dad named Mark took his eleven-year-old daughter on a daddy-daughter date to a drive-in movie. As they waited for the film to start, out of the blue she said, "Dad, it's kinda weird to think about who you're going to marry."

Mark nearly choked on his soft drink. He never expected a statement like that from his little girl. But there she was, moving beyond schoolyard chatter and starting a conversation about something *real*.

Mark quickly regained his composure. "Hmm. What kind of husband do you think God wants for you?"

Without hesitation, she began rattling off traits she felt were important in a husband. Clearly she had been thinking about this for a while. Wisely, Mark tried to keep listening and not critique her ideas too quickly. As the list grew, Mark came to a powerful and sobering realization: She was describing *him* and how he treats her mom.

Dad, that shouldn't be a surprise. You are a key role model for your little girl when it comes to the many aspects of manhood, including being a husband. She especially is watching you and filing away memories of what makes—or doesn't make—a good husband.

That concept should motivate us in several ways. As husbands, we need to recommit to being servant leaders and putting our bride's needs above our own. Divorced dads need to double their efforts to honor and respect their ex-wife. Respecting all women—refraining from coarse talk and refusing to objectify women—should be a priority. If your daughter has a brother, you may be tempted to engage in locker-room talk to gain his approval or show that you're "one of the guys." That's a losing proposition for every member of the family.

Take a moment to think of your daughter ten, fifteen, or twenty years from now. Your words and actions as a husband today may very well be reflected in her marriage. She's watching you when you're thoughtful, kind, and appreciative. She's also well aware of those times when you're angry, dismissive, and demanding.

Dad, go ahead and have high expectations for your future son-in-law. Your wonderful daughter deserves a wonderful guy. But also ask yourself if you are living up to those same high expectations right now in your marriage. No pressure.

And thanks to Mark for demonstrating one more reason why we need to date our daughters.[10]

"You have a little girl. An adorable little girl who looks up to you and adores you in a way you could never have imagined. I remember how her little hand used to fit inside mine. Then comes the day when she wants to get her ears pierced, and wants you to drop her off a block before the movie theater. From that moment on you're in a constant panic. You worry about her meeting the wrong kind of guy, the kind of guy who only wants one thing, and you know exactly what that one thing is, because it's the same thing you wanted when you were their age. Then, you stop worrying about her meeting the wrong guy, and you worry about her meeting the right guy. That's the greatest fear of all, because, then you lose her."

—George Banks
(Steve Martin, *Father of the Bride*, 1991)

Sing

Even men who don't sing may find themselves singing to a baby.

How about you? When you were changing your daughter's diaper or lying with her on the carpet, did you sing "Itsy-Bitsy Spider" or "Twinkle, Twinkle, Little Star"? Quite a few dads have discovered you can use an old pop song as a lullaby or father-daughter connecting point by slowing it down and singing with a gentle smile. Go ahead and try "I Gotta Feeling" from the Black-Eyed Peas or "Just the Way You Are" from Bruno Mars. (Or Billy Joel's song of the same name for that matter.) Quite a few U2 songs work as well—"With or Without You," "The Sweetest Thing," and "Beautiful Day."

And always feel free to sing any Beatles classics. Simply smile, coo, and sing.

Don't overlook contemporary Christian songs. I recommend you just go with your favorites. Some of mine are "Open the Eyes of My Heart," "I Can Only Imagine," and "Shine" by the Newsboys.

More than just singing to babies—which comes fairly easily—I recommend you continue singing to and with your growing daughter every chance you get. Sing her songs. Sing your songs. Sing show tunes. Sing TV theme songs. She enjoyed hearing you sing before she could even speak. You may not make it on *America's Got Talent*, but you'll make memories that can't be bought.

The test is when you and your daughter are in the car with one of her girlfriends. If a song you both like comes on the radio, will the two of you break out singing? Answer: probably not. She will be too embarrassed. But go for it anyway. She may roll her eyes and say, "Daa-aaad!" But secretly she'll be amused and even proud to have a dad who sings.

BIG IDEA 45

Take Advantage of the Local Daddy-Daughter Dance

Each year, park districts, schools, community centers, country clubs, and even churches around the country schedule something called the Daddy-Daughter Dance.

For the uninitiated, here's what you can expect. The events are just dads (and maybe some granddads or uncles) and their daughters up to about fifth grade. No moms or brothers allowed. The dads wear anything from nice shirts and slacks to tuxedos. My friend Gregg wore his best suit and tie and told me, "Lauren had the most beautiful dress and necklace Mom could have ever picked out for her. Her hair was done up perfectly."

You can be as formal and chivalrous as you want, but do

consider ringing your own doorbell, pinning on a corsage, posing for pictures, helping with her coat, opening car doors, and just being generally gallant. The dance probably will not include dinner but will likely have snacks and beverages. Bonus activities may include a magician or clown, balloon animals, complimentary photos, and party favors.

About the dance, Gregg remembers, "We walked in, arm in arm, and posed for pictures. What a special night. We had dinner at a fancy table, won door prizes, and danced the night away. Dads...you gotta dance!"

Gregg is exactly right. The highlight of the event is the dance itself—ninety minutes of songs you know and love that will have you and your daughter singing along and shaking your booties. Every town seems to have a DJ who specializes in daddy-daughter events and who knows how to get the crowd moving. The younger girls playfully swing on their daddy's arm or race around the floor. But the older girls— not quite young women—have a certain unspoken wistfulness about them as they know that childhood is coming to an end. The dads know that too. Often this will be the last time they dance together until her wedding reception, more than a decade away.

You will want to mentally prepare yourself to surrender to

the instructions of the DJ. Even if you're not a dancing kind of guy, getting out on the floor is an essential part of the evening. If you are instructed to put your right hip in and shake it all about, just do it. If a human locomotive chugs by, grab on. And please don't forget how to spell Y-M-C-A.

The evening will go by quickly. And so will the years. Pretty soon she'll be in middle school, way too mature for the organized daddy-daughter dance. When that happens, you will want to double your efforts to schedule intentional one-on-one dates with your blossoming daughter. Those dates probably will not include any dancing, but your conversation by candlelight may include some unexpected new information about what's going on in her life. You may even talk about boys, ambitions, and silly stuff that brothers and moms just don't get.[11]

Ten Dances to Do at a Daddy-Daughter Dance (Without Worrying About Being Embarrassed)

1. Chicken Dance
2. Macarena
3. Loco-Motion
4. Cha Cha Slide
5. any slow song during which you let her stand on your shoes
6. Butterfly Kisses
7. Bunny Hop
8. Twist
9. Hokey Pokey
10. YMCA

The New Cultural Expectations

What does the culture expect of this upcoming generation of growing girls?

Don't answer too fast. It may not be what you think. The presumption that women will find personal fulfillment staying home, cooking dinner, and making babies has fallen by the wayside.

Actually, in some circles, it's the exact opposite. A lamentable segment of the culture believes women who choose to be stay-at-home moms are failures. If they listen to those voices, bright young girls—like your daughter—will be saddled with a long list of crushing expectations that are virtually impossible to live up to. According to the push and pull of today's societal norms, your daughter has to achieve at a higher level than her male peers in every statistical category and look good doing it. Hair and makeup just right. Skinny. And always with a smile on her face.

I would call it an impossible task, but today's young women seem to be crushing it. According to a Pew Research Center report, females outpace males in college enrollment.[12] Women today earn the majority of college degrees, whether bachelor's, master's, or doctoral.[13] In 1998, just one woman led a *Fortune 500* company; by 2014, that number was up to twenty-four.[14] Furthermore, today's women are leading the way in these educational and professional advancements while surrendering allegiance to the impossible standards of beauty established by the $230 billion cosmetics industry.[15]

The unavoidable conclusion is this: Your daughter needs to be brilliant, crash through glass ceilings, achieve fame and fortune, and look fabulous. *Or does she?*

Is your daughter required to meet the burdensome pronouncements of today's culture? If God wired her to be a corporate tycoon, Olympic champion, presidential hopeful, or Academy Award–winning actress, that's awesome. Come alongside her and cheer her on.

But just as awesome is the idea that the plan for her life is far different from the expectations established by the media and cultural elite. In her heart of hearts, your daughter might want to be married or single, to be a mom or a missionary, to do something that seemingly impacts only her small corner of the world, or maybe even to follow in her daddy's footsteps.

So don't let your daughter submit blindly to the expectations of the world—the new expectations or the old ones. And make sure you don't burden your little girl with any of your own demanding paternal expectations...except one. Convey with love and humility to your maturing daughter the expectation and rewards of trusting God and seeking his will.

Psalm 37 says it well. "Commit your way to the LORD; trust in him and he will do this: He will make your righteous reward shine like the dawn, your vindication like the noonday sun" (verses 5-6).

Walking in the way of the Lord. Shining like the dawn. For your daughter, that's a brilliant and fabulous existence that will last for eternity. [16]

The School Lunch Break

This works at any age from kindergarten through high school. Arrange to pick your daughter up from school exactly when her lunch period begins and get her back before the first afternoon bell. Take her somewhere close and quick where you can sit in a booth. You'll probably have less than an hour. There doesn't have to be any specific agenda. It's just a time for you to check in and for her to feel special.

Some things to consider. Plan ahead a few days. Don't make it a surprise. Often a school lunch hour is important socially or academically. Your daughter may not want to miss an ongoing bit of drama with her lunch table chums or a meeting scheduled with an advisor or teacher. There may also be some competition or program going on in the schoolyard that she doesn't want to miss. On any given day, things go on during lunch *besides* lunch.

On the other hand, your daughter's absence may be quite noticeable to her peers. They'll all want to know where she was for that forty-five minutes, and they'll all be jealous of her date with her dad. Another benefit of stealing away your daughter during her school day is that you don't have to think of topics to cover hours of conversation. The short lunch hour will pass quickly without a single awkward pause.

Every school is different, so you'll want to make sure you abide by school policies. What door to use? Is there a sign-out sheet? Where can you park? Do you need a name tag or escort to walk through the building? School security has gotten tighter in the last generation, and you'll want to honor the rules. The best strategy is to call the school secretary and ask her advice. She should be more than happy to help a dad connect with his daughter.

If you're a little hesitant, you may want to initiate your daddy-daughter lunch tradition on or near your daughter's birthday. That's an easier call to make. "Hi, this is Kelly's dad. I'd like to take her out of school for lunch on her birthday next Tuesday. What's the school policy?"

After you've sneaked her out of school once, it'll be much easier in the future. Even as she moves on to middle school and high school and beyond. Who knows? You may have regular stolen lunch hours with your daughter for decades to come.

Affirm Your Daughter's Existence

You can probably skip this Big Idea. But there is a chance you're carrying an attitude or demeanor that can be seriously damaging to your perfect little girl. It shows up in men who wanted a son and got a daughter. Or got several daughters.

Of course, the desire to have a son is not the problem. I dare say, at some point, most expectant fathers imagine what it would be like to have a son and raise him in their manly ways.

But when that little girl arrives, love takes over. There's an overwhelming flood of joy, awe, and pride. Your paternal instincts kick in. You decide, *That little bitty baby girl is going to have the best dad ever!* A father committed to his daughter and earning her trust can build one of the most beautiful relationships in the world.

But some dads hold back. They don't let themselves surrender to the blessings and rewards of being the father of a little girl. And she will pick up on that. Maybe it starts when the new baby first arrives and he doesn't hold her as much. As she gets older, he doesn't tickle or nuzzle her, swoop her around, or get down on the carpet and engage her as much. Later, that daughter hears her father joke about not understanding females or turn down invitations because he says, "I don't do girl stuff." Once in a while, he may begin a sentence with "If you were a boy..."

This is a hard question that needs to be asked: Dad, is there a chance that your daughter—even though she feels your love—still has a nagging sense that her arrival on earth was cause for disappointment?

This is a good time to remind *all* dads that you need to make sure *all* your kids know how much they are loved, cherished, adored, and worthy of affection. If you've been neglectful in that regard, I recommend you overstate the obvious to make sure they truly understand they are valued gifts from God. Especially tell your daughter she is the delight of your life and when you think of her, you are overwhelmed with gratitude and can't stop smiling.

Got it? Well, here are two more thoughts.

First, if one of your daughters goes through a tomboy phase, just go with it. (I'm not sure they use the term "tomboy" anymore, but you get the idea.) There's a special place in a father's heart for a little girl who climbs trees, loves competition, and stands up for herself. Enjoy it. Come alongside her as she makes some unexpected choices. Follow her lead. Let her passions guide her. She may go through a few different seasons of life as she figures out her priorities. Be ready for anything—along the way she may even ask your advice.

Second, if you keep pouring into the life of your daughter, staying close, and serving as a role model for how a good husband looks and acts, she may someday bring home a guy just like you. And you'll get a sharp, engaging son-in-law out of the deal. That young man will be glad you raised your little girl exactly the way you did.

Ten Scripture Verses for Your Daughter

1. "Do not conform to the pattern of this world" (Romans 12:2).

2. "Don't let anyone think less of you because you are young. Be an example to all believers in what you say, in the way you live, in your love, your faith, and your purity" (1 Timothy 4:12 NLT).

3. "Weeping may last through the night, but joy comes with the morning" (Psalm 30:5 NLT).

4. "Everything is possible for one who believes" (Mark 9:23).

5. "You created my inmost being; you knit me together in my mother's womb. I praise you because I am fearfully and wonderfully made; your works are wonderful, I know that full well" (Psalm 139:13-14).

6. "The heart is deceitful above all things" (Jeremiah 17:9).

7. "From everyone who has been given much, much will be demanded" (Luke 12:48).

8. "Those unwilling to work will not get to eat" (2 Thessalonians 3:10 NLT).

9. "Charm is deceptive, and beauty is fleeting; but a woman who fears the Lord is to be praised" (Proverbs 31:30).

10. "The fear of the Lord is the beginning of knowledge" (Proverbs 1:7).

Bake

My friend Mitch has a twenty-five-year-old daughter. For as long as she can remember, they've been baking partners. For a while it was mostly store-bought mixes and Toll House cookie recipes. Then they started getting a bit more creative. Baking from scratch and trying new recipes. The results are fabulous desserts, creative cooperation, and lots of laughter and memory making. Recipes that totally flopped or burned to a crisp turned out to be especially valuable, providing fewer calories and sweeter memories.

As you can imagine, the rest of the family is appreciative of these baking partners and the fruits of their labor. Mitch recommends the idea to dads everywhere. He and his daughter now email each other recipes, planning for their next kitchen-based mission.

Baking is one of those activities that puts you and your daughter in close proximity, but there's no pressure to have to come up with topics of conversation. You're baking! And talking about baking. If something needs to be said, the kitchen is a safe place to say it. Making a mess is part of the process. Cleaning up builds teamwork. And afterward, there's cake.

In case you were wondering, Mitch reports a good bit of flour has been scattered on occasion, but so far, no pie fights.

Ten Recipes to Try with Your Daughter

1. Toll House cookies

2. pigs in a blanket

3. chicken soup with rice
(in honor of the Maurice Sendak book)

4. green eggs and ham
(in honor of the Dr. Seuss book)

5. birthday cake for Mom

6. odd-shaped pancakes (created by squirting batter
on the griddle with a turkey baster)

7. healthy fruit and kale shakes in the blender

8. classic mac and cheese

9. any Thanksgiving side dish
(acknowledged with pride as the serving dish
is passed around the table)

10. pizza with everything

Be Her Biggest Fan

Consider this Big Idea a reminder and warning of how the mind of a middle schooler works. Actually, for girls, this thought process may begin in fourth or fifth grade.

Your daughter will be sitting in a classroom, look around, and suddenly think everyone is better than her. For that moment—or maybe that entire school year—she will believe she has fallen behind in school, sports, fashion, and physical appearance.

You need to hope she comes to you with those feelings. If she goes to some other source, she may hear words that further crush her spirit or lead to long-term feelings of inadequacy. Or she may get awful advice, enticing her to make up for her supposed deficiencies in terrible ways.

If she comes to you, cracks open the door to her heart, and reveals some of those emotions, handle with care. Listen for as long as she keeps speaking. Don't minimize what she's feeling. Don't say, "That's silly, Chloe! You are beautiful and perfect and smart and the best athlete in that school!" Because she will know your words are not entirely true.

What can you say? Whatever you say, make sure it's rooted in truth. And it's always a good idea to match her emotions. If she's sad, be a little sad. If she's angry, be just a little angry yourself. If she's worried, let her know that's okay too. Then quietly say something like this.

"Chloe...I'm so glad we're talking. There's a lot going on...things you've been thinking about for a while and new stuff too. I don't see everything and I can't fix everything, but I'm here for you. Always. You're growing up and there's hard stuff...and stuff you miss from when you were little...and stuff that's scary. Here's what I know for sure. There are amazing things right around the corner for you...fun things, challenges, friends, stuff that's a little scary...and you are more than ready. I know I'm your dad and you may not believe everything I say, but when I look at you, I see someone with so much to give...a kind heart, someone who's thoughtful and fun to be with...a girl with dreams and a future filled with all kinds of possibilities. Many you haven't even thought of yet. God has some crazy cool plans for you...I can't wait to see how he uses you...maybe sooner than you think. And you *are* beautiful...inside and out...so...keep doing what you're doing. Don't be afraid to try new things...some things will be hard, and some things will be easy for you that are hard for someone else. Chloe, I love you so much...more than you know...let's keep checking in with each other."

Now, I know this sounds like the last two minutes of an episode of *Full House*. The corny music starts and Danny, Uncle Jesse, or even D.J. gives a little speech, and all the conflict and worries are whisked away before the commercial break. Well, the truth is that words can hurt and words can heal. Your availability and presence, along with a few well-chosen words, can provide some much-needed encouragement. (Notice the root word, "courage.") Your job, Dad, is to listen well, acknowledge her emotions, confirm your availability, offer an optimistic long-term view, and be her biggest cheerleader. Not the loudest, but the one she trusts the most.

After your little speech, feel free to ask a question or two. Something like, "What's the biggest thing on your mind right now?" Or "How can I pray for you?" Then keep listening. Believe it or not, someday you'll miss these conversations.

"No one in this world can love a girl more than her father."

—Michael Ratnadeepak

BIG IDEA 51

The Big Talk

There's a time and place for big talks. Occasionally you or her mother (or both of you) need to sit down with your daughter and have reasonably long, intentional talks about real-life issues, like table manners, God's grace, boys and dating, sexual purity, study habits, drugs and alcohol, choosing a college or career, and the responsibilities that come with a new driver's license.

But big talks with your daughter shouldn't occur in a vacuum. They're not stand-alone, one-time lectures. Big talks need context. Without a doubt, you have much to teach your daughter about surviving this world and thriving in the next. But without having established a solid relationship, big talks will fall on deaf ears. So starting at a young age, your daughter should be part of a family culture that includes good role models, personal discipline, frequent Q&A initiated by parents, frequent Q&A initiated by your daughter, and lots of hanging out together.

One of my favorite parenting verses in the Bible is from the Old Testament:

> These commandments that I give you today are to be on your hearts. Impress them on your children. Talk about them when you sit at home and when you walk along the road, when you lie down and when you get up (Deuteronomy 6:6-7).

This passage explains the ideal strategy for passing on your hard-earned knowledge, moral code, and spiritual beliefs. Don't wait for just the right moment or the perfectly planned weekend to deliver a big talk in a single grandiose and laborious speech.

Instead, gently and consistently "impress them on your children." Notice that the command isn't to bash them over the head or screech into their cranium. It doesn't say nag, cajole, or fume. The word "impress" suggests images of a dad lovingly leaving an imprint in his daughter's life. Almost like an artist signing a fine oil painting. Girls respond very well to this kind of relationship building.

How does a dad do this? Go back to the passage. Talk to them during the regular course of life. At the kitchen table. During commercial breaks. Strolling around the block. Tucking them in at night. Chatting over waffles.

Make life an ongoing conversation. If a question comes up you can't answer, that's okay. They know you'll weave in and out of their day with fresh insight, thought-provoking follow up, and a listening ear. When it's time for one of those big talks, you'll get fewer confused looks and more nodding heads.

The Business Trip Tag Along

If business or ministry trips take you away from home on a regular basis, it only seems fair that some of those trips provide opportunities to bring your family closer. So if you can work out the details, take your daughter on a business trip. Really.

Of course, you can't just toss a child in your suitcase. And you can't expect the company to pick up the tab. But it may be easier than you think. Your organization may already have a policy in place. And in general, management knows that good dads make good employees.

One thing not to stress about is having your daughter miss a couple days of school. Your daughter will learn more during an adventure with you than she will in a typical week at school. Any good teacher would celebrate a chance for a student to spend a few days with her dad.

You'll have to work out the details regarding where your daughter stays when you're doing your actual work. Depending on her age and the nature of your work, she may even be an asset to your business trip. If you can tag a vacation day on to your travels, even better.

If your job never takes you out of town, count your blessings. My friend Tom suggests you bring your daughter to work once a year or so, giving her a chance to see that side of your life. Families who homeschool, dads who work for themselves, and stay-at-home dads can apply the business trip idea in their own creative ways. Regardless of how you help her enter your world, she'll have a new appreciation for who you are and what you do to support the family.

Reflect Back

One of the most compelling strategies I've ever come across for helping your daughter recognize and even celebrate her positive capabilities comes from a book by Michelle Watson that I highly recommend: *Dad, Here's What I Really Need from You*. The author links your intentional, verbal engagement with your daughter's self-image. The strategy is not difficult and is undeniably self-evident. Why don't we do this?

- If you laugh at her jokes, she tells herself, *I'm funny.*

- If you discuss politics and world events with her, she tells herself, *I'm interesting.*

- If you draw her out, asking her opinion about a fact, theory, or line of thought, she tells herself, *I'm knowledgeable.*

- If you ask for her help to fix something, she tells herself, *I'm capable.*

- If you ask her to help you brainstorm about buying a present for Mom, she tells herself, *I'm clever.*

- If you applaud her for her achievements in sports, grades, music or work, she tells herself, *I'm competent.*

- If you enthusiastically affirm her artistic endeavors, she tells herself, *I'm creative.*

- If you celebrate her academic prowess, she tells herself, *I'm smart.*

- If you actively listen to her while she is talking, she tells herself, *I'm engaging.*

- If you teach her to say no and then respect her boundaries, she tells herself, *I'm strong.*

- If you light up and smile when she walks in the room, she tells herself, *I'm delightful.*

- If you respect her opinions about topics ranging from literature to spiritual things, she tells herself, *I'm wise.*

- If you treat her with kindness, understanding, tenderness, and love, she tells herself, *I'm worthy.*

By the way, Dr. Watson states these truths positively, but they can also be turned around. Consider this disturbing but accurate statement: If you dismiss or ignore your daughter when she attempts to talk to you, she tells herself, *I'm boring and have nothing to offer.*

So. What are you reflecting back to your daughter?[17]

Ten Things You Never Experienced That Your Daughter Will

1. Dotting a lowercase "i" with a heart or flower.

2. An obsessive desire to dye your hair.

3. Asking someone to accompany you to the bathroom.

4. Changing clothes seventeen times before a date.

5. Paying $115 for a haircut.

6. Being the only person of your gender in a science club or computer programming class.

7. Worrying about spotting on your favorite blue jeans.

8. Being bullied or mocked in middle school because your breasts were too big or too small.

9. Pretending to be dumb because you didn't want to be labeled a brainiac.

10. Worrying about wearing the wrong kind, wrong color, or wrong amount of eyeliner, blush, or mascara.

Clear Her for Competition

It may be natural for you to encourage your son to compete. But your daughter...not so much. That's a glitch you can fix pretty efficiently. And you should.

Competition helps young people compare themselves to their peers. While some may suggest that comparison is the source of all kinds of negative emotions, I fall in another camp. Competition (and thereby comparison) reveals your daughter's weaknesses and strengths. Knowing what you're good at—compared to your peers—helps develop self-confidence and guides you toward hobbies, sports, classes, college majors, and careers in which you might find success.

You can't count on schools to motivate your daughter to compete. Competition is seriously frowned upon these days.

For girls and boys. A generation ago, part of the classroom experience was spelling bees, geography bees, dictionary races, book reading contests, and memorization competition. Teachers even dared post the best artwork and cleverest science project in a classroom showcase. Today, school administrators tend to downplay children's various levels of talent, skill, giftedness, perseverance, and experience. When this happens, instead of encouraging excellence, they applaud mediocrity.

I encourage you to ask your daughter whether she ever has any legitimate opportunities to compete. Make it a topic of conversation. Talk about your own wins and losses over the years. Include examples of organized activities and games, races, and rivalries that naturally occurred in the course of life.

If your daughter prefers to stand and chat with friends on the playground, that's fine. She's building other skills that come in handy. But she should know that it's okay to participate in a spontaneous game of tag, four square, or kickball. And if a courageous teacher goes retro and dares to hold a spelling bee, then she should spell boldly without fear. Girls need to know that being smart, competitive, and goal-oriented are worthy and enviable character traits.

Raise your daughter to be an active participant in life and not just watch the world pass by without digging deep and investing in a worthy cause. Competition doesn't just teach children how to compete. It teaches them who they are and whom they might become.

"Believe me, the reward is not so great without the struggle."

—Wilma Rudolph

Make Your Home a Hangout

You want your little girl to be safe and supervised. One of the best ways to assure that happens is to make your home a comfortable and inviting place for all kids. Even the ones you're not sure about. (*Especially* the ones you're not sure about.)

Keep soda in the fridge and chips in the cabinet. Put a Ping-Pong table in the basement. Establish a place where kids can play video and karaoke games. The goal is to create a comfort zone in your home where your daughter and friends hang out with just enough privacy to talk, laugh, share secrets, and make lifelong connections. Establish a pattern allowing you to enter or pass through that space without too much of an apology. If you have a bag of Dilly Bars or a bowl of popcorn, that makes it even easier.

We have a fire pit in our backyard where scores of kids have gathered after football games and youth group events. We even have a designated shelf in our kitchen for graham crackers, marshmallows, and Hershey bars. Sometimes I will mosey out and join the conversation around the campfire. Most of the time, we give the kids their space.

The knowledge we gain is worth the effort. We know where our kids are. We know who their friends are. Just hearing snippets of conversations reveals much about how young people make choices and what is important to them.

Making your home a hangout also establishes that Mom and Dad's house is a place where adult kids are always welcome and will feel comfortable and have fun. And maybe they'll even bring grandkids someday.

When You and Your Daughter Hit a Roadblock

You may be navigating a difficult situation right now—zero communication, harsh words, fear, anger, helplessness. Even so, don't give up on the future. As your daughter matures, she's going to come across new ideas and new challenges that may conflict with your way of thinking. As she sorts out her priorities and opinions, you may be tempted to step away. Please don't. She actually needs you in her life more than ever.

The fastest pathway to reconciliation is probably up to you. Take a hard look at what triggered that father-daughter conflict and see if you can look at the situation from her perspective. Don't sacrifice your core values, but if you said or did something for which you need to apologize, do it.

If you're at a standoff and you're waiting for your daughter to break down and make reparations, you may be waiting for a long time. As motivation for you to take the first step toward reconciliation, I encourage you to consider some of the enjoyable and rewarding events—both small and large—you might miss if you allow the clash of wills to go too long.

- Sitting together with your daughter on the couch, watching an old movie.

- Helping her move into a dorm room or apartment.

- Applauding when she receives her diploma.

- Hearing her ask your advice about a problem at work.

- Taking her out for a nice dinner to celebrate a new job, a promotion, an opening night, a presidential appointment, a million-dollar signing bonus, an early parole, or a year's sobriety.

- Seeing your little girl find just the right husband.

- Walking her down the aisle.
- Scraping up a few extra bucks to help pay for her wedding. (Consider it a privilege!)
- Welcoming grandkids.
- Being called "Gramps" or "Papa" or "G-Daddy."
- Going to school concerts, ballgames, and carnivals with your grandkids.
- Enjoying your daughter's presence as she cares for you in your old age.
- Having your daughter with you in heaven.

Every season of life comes with events and milestones you don't want to miss. If your daughter freezes you out—or vice versa—you'll miss new opportunities to hang out, laugh, create memories, build trust, and respectfully challenge each other's opinions. You won't always agree. But you can agree that you make each other wiser, stronger, more thoughtful, and more valuable to the world.

When the sparring is done—or between rounds—you may even get her to admit that the two of you make a pretty good team.

"If we don't start trusting our children...how will they ever become trustworthy? I'm told that the senior class at the high school...has gotten use of the warehouse in Bayson...for the purpose of putting on a senior dance. Please...join me to pray to the Lord to guide them in their endeavors."

—Reverend Shaw Moore
(John Lithgow, *Footloose*, 1984)

Pray for Her Future Husband

One of the most surreal experiences for any dad is praying for his daughter's future husband. You're praying for an individual you probably haven't met yet.

Or maybe you have. Your little girl may end up marrying the goofy-looking little boy from her pre-K Sunday school class. (Who turns out very handsome, by the way.) Or she might end up catching the eye of her older brother's best friend, who has been hanging around your house for years.

Praying for your daughter's future husband can lead to real blessings. You'll want to begin even before she shows any real interest in dating. That way she's not thinking of specific boys, and you're demonstrating that you care about her future. Not just guiding her through school and into a career, but more importantly, equipping her for meaningful adult relationships. Part of your job is to teach her how to love, forgive, listen, care, be tender, be tough, sacrifice, and put other people's needs before her own.

When you pray for her future husband, you're laying the foundation for your daughter to be a godly wife—if that's what God calls her to be, which is an interesting point. That child you're praying for may be called to singleness. And that has to be okay.

Paul remained single and saw it as a gift. In 1 Corinthians 7:7-8, he takes a moment from his instructions to married people to give a sincere shout-out to individuals who are called to singleness: "I wish that all of you were as I am. But each of you has your own gift from God; one has this gift, another has that. Now to the unmarried and the widows I say: It is good for them to stay unmarried, as I do."

In recent years, as my four sons announced their engagements, Rita and I had the delightful privilege to tell Lindsay, Rachel, Megan, and Kaitlin that we had been praying for them for years. Not praying that our sons would each find a wife. We were praying for those four young ladies as individuals. Rita and I prayed that God would protect these girls as they grew into young women and prepare their hearts to be united with our sons.

Dad, I encourage you to lift up this prayer in private and also *with your daughter*. But be careful not to put expectations on her. She doesn't have to get married. And she certainly doesn't have to marry the first boy who catches her eye. Starting when she's still in elementary school, have lots of age-appropriate conversations about love, marriage, sex, and what to look for in a spouse. Make it a point to close those conversations with prayer. Pray that your daughter hears, understands, and surrenders to God's will. Pray for God's protection on that boy who *may* be out there, whom God *may* be preparing to be a lifelong marriage partner for your little girl.

Ten Father of the Bride Songs

1. "Unforgettable"
Natalie Cole with Nat King Cole

2. "Isn't She Lovely?"
Stevie Wonder

3. "Somewhere over the Rainbow"
Israel "IZ" Kamakawiwoʻole

4. "In My Life"
The Beatles

5. "Cinderella"
Steven Curtis Chapman

6. "What a Wonderful World"
Louis Armstrong

7. "Lullabye (Goodnight, My Angel)"
Billy Joel

8. "I Loved Her First"
   Heartland

9. "Through the Years"
   Kenny Rogers

10. "Butterfly Kisses"
    Bob Carlisle

Love Her Now

Take it from a dad with five kids, all of whom are just about grown and gone. It really does go by so fast. At one point, you held that little baby girl and wondered how you could possibly know what to do over the next twenty years. Then suddenly you're looking back and wondering how those two decades vanished so quickly.

One of the reasons the years flash by is that you're doing double, triple, or quadruple duty. You may be a father, husband, breadwinner, and man of faith. All at the same time. There are only 168 hours in a week, and you don't want to disappoint your daughter, bride, boss, or God. So you find yourself attempting to multitask. You're crunching on a work deadline, but your mind drifts to your next family outing.

You sneak out of your daughter's oboe recital to check an email from a client. You're having a romantic dinner with your wife, but the sole topic of conversation is your daughter's silly fight with her girlfriend.

Because you're pulled in so many directions, no one is getting your best effort. And life gets even more blurry. What to do?

First, lose the guilt. Dad, even if you've missed ten critical items on your calendar this month, it never helps to beat yourself up.

Second, try to focus on the task at hand. It may help to remember that God wrote, "Whatever your hand finds to do, do it with all your might" (Ecclesiastes 9:10). That tells you that God is pleased when you are giving 110 percent to whatever is right in front of you. So in the moment, simply be the best employee, dad, or husband you can be. That idea should relieve some of the pressure and stop you from trying to do more than is humanly possible.

Third, don't let the busyness of life rob you of the joy. Psalm 127 tells us, "Children are a gift from the LORD; they are a reward from him" (verse 3 NLT). Kids are not a burden. Your daughter's time at home is not a season you're hoping to survive. Savor every day as an opportunity, a gift, and a blessing. That frame of mind should be your goal. If you open your heart, that sentiment will be a sure guide.

Every time you think about your daughter, you smile. Right? Even if she's been a royal pain recently. She will always be one of your greatest joys. There is nothing you wouldn't do for her. Without hesitation, you would trade your life for hers.

So here's your final Big Idea. Don't die for her; live with her. When she's little, be nose to nose. Memorize her face so you can know instantly when something just isn't right. When she smiles, smile back. When she frowns, frown back. When she learns something new, celebrate with her. When she stumbles, offer a hand or a hug. Memorize the color of her eyes and the length of her lashes.

Then after years of being nose to nose, turn ever so slightly so that the two of you are shoulder to shoulder. Still connected. Still tight. But now you're helping her see into the future. It's a bright one that your daughter will enter with confidence and conviction. Because that little girl grew up with a dad who loved her then, loves her now, and will love her always.

"Well, I guess there's one problem left...How much I'm going to miss her."

—King Triton
(Kenneth Mars, *The Little Mermaid*, 1989)

Daddy-Daughter Dates to Complete and Chronicle

In the next year or so, see if you can journal the date, location, and a brief memory from twenty or thirty dates with your daughter. Don't feel like you have to do everything. Accept it as a joy-filled challenge. Some of these outings take significant planning, and some you can do on the spur of the moment. Use this list for inspiration and as a reminder that your little girl will be this age for just a little while.

Keep this list handy. Add your own ideas and destinations.

Go window shopping.

_____

date   *location*

_____

a memory...

Mini golf.

_____
date   location

_____
a memory…

Real golf at a par-three course or your favorite club.

_____
date   location

_____
a memory…

Visit a museum.

_____
date   location

_____
a memory…

Visit an arboretum, antique village, or Renaissance faire.

_____

date   *location*

_____

a memory...

Visit a pet store. Pet a puppy, talk to a parrot, or buy a reptile without Mom's permission.

_____

date   *location*

_____

a memory...

Take her to lunch. Arrange to pick her up from school and get her back before afternoon classes.

_____

date   *location*

_____

a memory...

Visit a nearby college campus. Talk about the future.

_____

date   *location*

_____

a memory...

Do something girls do with their moms, like pottery, painting, or jewelry making.

_____

date   *location*

_____

a memory...

A midnight movie.

_____

date   *location*

_____

a memory...

Go apple picking. Make a pie.

_____

date   *location*

_____

a memory...

Try sushi. (Or some other dish neither of you have
ever sampled.)

_____

date   *location*

_____

a memory...

Go ice skating.

_____

date   *location*

_____

a memory...

Ride go-karts.

_____

date   _location_

_____

a memory...

Buy and boil a lobster.

_____

date   _location_

_____

a memory...

Make a pizza from scratch.

_____

date   _location_

_____

a memory...

Go horseback riding.

_____

date   *location*

_____

a memory...

Go paintballing.

_____

date   *location*

_____

a memory...

Go to an NFL, NBA, NHL, or MLB game. Take a selfie with the game action behind you.

_____

date   *location*

_____

a memory...

Go on a double date with your daughter's best friend and her dad.

_____

date   *location*

_____

a memory...

Go the bank and start a savings account. Give her $100!

_____

date   *location*

_____

a memory...

Walk around a cemetery. Maybe visit a relative's grave site.

_____

date   *location*

_____

a memory...

Wash and vacuum Mom's car.

_____

date   *location*

_____

a memory...

Bowling.

_____

date   *location*

_____

a memory...

Birdwatching.

_____

date   *location*

_____

a memory...

See a ballet or modern dance concert.

_____

date   _location_

_____

a memory...

Visit an art fair or gallery.

_____

date   _location_

_____

a memory...

Browse a bookstore. Buy a book to read together.

_____

date   _location_

_____

a memory...

Take a yoga class together.

_____

date   *location*

_____

a memory...

Sing a karaoke duet.

_____

date   *location*

_____

a memory...

Do a random act of kindness.

_____

date   *location*

_____

a memory...

Tie-dye T-shirts.

_____

date   *location*

_____

a memory...

Banana splits!

_____

date   *location*

_____

a memory...

Road trip!

_____

date   *location*

_____

a memory...

What else?

_____

date   *location*

_____

a memory...

Something really silly.

_____

date   *location*

_____

a memory...

Your daughter's choice!

_____

date   *location*

_____

a memory...

NOTES

1. Adapted from Jay Payleitner, Brock Griffin, and Carey Casey, *It's Great Being a Dad* (Eugene: Harvest House, 2015), 18-19.

2. Adapted from Jay Payleitner, *52 Things Daughters Need from Their Dads* (Eugene: Harvest House, 2013), 124.

3. Adapted from *52 Things Daughters Need from Their Dads*, 34.

4. Adapted from *52 Things Daughters Need from Their Dads*, 55.

5. Meg Meeker, *Strong Fathers, Strong Daughters* (Washington DC: Regnery Publishing, 2006), 129-30.

6. Adapted from *52 Things Daughters Need from Their Dads*, 14.

7. Erin Ollila, "Top 15 Best Selling Toys in History," *Blitz*, June 13, 2016, www.nowblitz.com/blog/15-best-selling-toys-in-history/.

8. Adapted from *52 Things Daughters Need from Their Dads*, 28.

9. Adapted from *It's Great Being a Dad*, 82-83.

10. Adapted from *It's Great Being a Dad*, 74-75.

11. Adapted from Jay Payleitner, *52 Things Kids Need from a Dad* (Eugene: Harvest House, 2010), 133.

12. Mark Hugo Lopez and Ana Gonzalez-Barrera, "Women's college enrollment gains leave men behind," *Pew Research Center*, March 6, 2014, http://www.pewresearch.org/fact-tank/2014/03/06/womens -college-enrollment-gains-leave-men-behind/.

13. Jeff Guo, "Women are dominating men at college. Blame Sexism," *The Washington Post*, December 11, 2014, https://www.washington post.com/news/storyline/wp/2014/12/11/women-are-dominating -men-at-college-blame-sexism/.

14. Caroline Fairchild, "Number of Fortune 500 women CEOs reaches historic high," *Fortune*, June 3, 2014, http://fortune.com/2014/06/03/ number-of-fortune-500-women-ceos-reaches-historic-high/.

15. Mmoma Ejiofor, "World's Best-Selling Makeup," *Forbes*, February 9, 2006, http://www.forbes.com/2006/02/08/best-selling-cosmetics _cx_me_0209feat_ls.html.

16. Adapted from *52 Things Daughters Need from Their Dads*, 131-32.

17. Adapted from Michelle Watson, *Dad, Here's What I Really Need from You* (Eugene: Harvest House, 2014), 51-52.

ACKNOWLEDGMENTS

Thanks for inspiration from all the girls I love so much, including...

My beautiful and multi-talented daughter, Rae Anne.

My exquisite daughters-in-law, Lindsay, Rachel, Megan, and Kaitlin.

My perfect granddaughters, Emerson and Reese.

My warmhearted sisters, Mary Kay and Sue.

My patient bride, Rita.

Thanks to the dads and moms who contributed directly to these Big Ideas, including Dave George, Tom Chilton, Matt Haviland, Mitch Belon, Chad and Chassyn Gasper, Gregg Brusven, and Michelle Watson.

Thanks to the team at Harvest House, who continue to challenge me to do work that matters, especially Gene Skinner, Kyle Hatfield, and Barb Sherrill.

Thanks to any dad who continually pursues ideas on how to best love on his little girl no matter how old she is. Your daughter is counting on you.

ABOUT THE AUTHOR

Prior to becoming a full-time author and speaker, **Jay Payleitner** served as freelance radio producer for a wide range of international movements, including the Salvation Army, Prison Fellowship, Bible League, Voice of the Martyrs, and National Center for Fathering.

Jay is a family advocate, life pundit, and humorist. His books, including *52 Things Kids Need from a Dad*, *The Dad Manifesto*, and *What If God Wrote Your Bucket List?* have sold more than half a million copies and have been translated into French, German, Spanish, Slovenian, and Russian.

Jay is a national speaker for conferences, retreats, and weekend services with messages on parenting, marriage, creativity, storytelling, and finding your life purpose. He has been a guest multiple times on *The Harvest Show*, *100 Huntley Street*, and *Focus on the Family*. Jay also served as executive director of the Illinois Fatherhood Initiative.

Jay and his high school sweetheart, Rita, live in the Chicago area, where they raised five great kids, loved on ten foster babies, and are cherishing grandparenthood. Jay and Rita's daughter, Rae Anne, attended West Point and University College Dublin and is currently working on her first novel. There's much more at JayPayleitner.com.

MORE GREAT HARVEST HOUSE BOOKS

by Jay Payleitner

For dads…

10 Conversations Kids Need to Have with Their Dad
365 Ways to Say "I Love You" to Your Kids
52 Things Daughters Need from Their Dads
52 Things Kids Need from a Dad
52 Things Sons Need from Their Dads
52 Things to Pray for Your Kids
The Dad Book
The Dad Manifesto
It's Great Being a Dad

For husbands…

52 Things Husbands Need from Their Wives
52 Things Wives Need from Their Husbands
52 Ways to Connect as a Couple

For all men…

What If God Wrote Your Bucket List?